The Machine Shed Roots

We opened the Iowa Machine Shed Restaurant in 1978 in rural Davenport, Iowa with just over 100 seats. Our location wasn't great and much of the equipment was old (but clean) and broke too often.

We were all pretty young and green. But we started with a powerful commitment; that commitment was a simple five word constitution- "Dedicated to the Iowa Farmer." That dedication meant that we worked to have a restaurant that wasn't just "farm" themed but would be something that farmers could be proud of. That meant using only the best pork and beef, real whipped cream on the pies, hearty soups, fresh baked goods made from scratch, and little things like genuine mashed potatoes and real butter. Although we still had a lot to learn, that dedication guided us through the early days. Even though money was tight, we were never tempted to take a cheaper route.

Thanks to you, folks like The Machine Shed from the start. The original Machine shed has been expanded and improved many times. And now, other Machine Sheds have sprung up in Des Moines, Iowa; Olathe, Kansas; Rockford Illinois; Pewaukee and Appleton, Wisconsin. Along the way we have been delighted to have received a bushel basketful of honors from farm groups like the Pork Producers and the Beef Industry Council. We're constantly trying to live up to those honors on the food we prepare and in the way we prepare and the way we bring it to you.

Mike Whalen

Thanks for your help

Heart of America

Restaurants & Inns™
True midwestern hospitality
Visit all of Heart of America's properties throughout the midwest

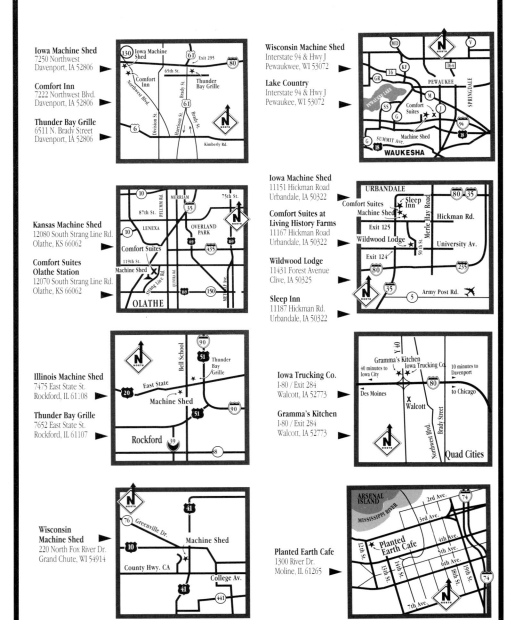

Iowa Machine Shed
7250 Northwest
Davenport, IA 52806

Comfort Inn
7222 Northwest Blvd.
Davenport, IA 52806

Thunder Bay Grille
6511 N. Brady Street
Davenport, IA 52806

Kansas Machine Shed
12080 South Strang Line Rd.
Olathe, KS 66062

Comfort Suites Olathe Station
12070 South Strang Line Rd.
Olathe, KS 66062

Illinois Machine Shed
7475 East State St.
Rockford, IL 61108

Thunder Bay Grille
7652 East State St.
Rockford, IL 61107

Wisconsin Machine Shed
220 North Fox River Dr.
Grand Chute, WI 54914

Wisconsin Machine Shed
Interstate 94 & Hwy J
Pewaukee, WI 53072

Lake Country
Interstate 94 & Hwy J
Pewaukee, WI 53072

Iowa Machine Shed
11151 Hickman Road
Urbandale, IA 50322

Comfort Suites at Living History Farms
11167 Hickman Road
Urbandale, IA 50322

Wildwood Lodge
11431 Forest Avenue
Clive, IA 50325

Sleep Inn
11187 Hickman Rd.
Urbandale, IA 50322

Iowa Trucking Co.
I-80 / Exit 284
Walcott, IA 52773

Gramma's Kitchen
I-80 / Exit 284
Walcott, IA 52773

Planted Earth Cafe
1300 River Dr.
Moline, IL 61265

There is a growing trend in our country to get back to the basics of gardening, harvesting and processing our own crops. In this book you will find monthly gardening tips supplied by Master Gardener, **Lois Jakoby**, aided by the Peoria County *Master Gardeners' Gazette.*

To utilize your abundant harvest, freezing and canning tips have been designed and refined by our favorite food enthusiast, **Mary Schneckloth**. Those of you familiar with Mary's recipes will be eager to devour this latest collection which includes light picnic fare and great grilling ideas.

You will find yourself referring back to this book over and over again. Share a copy with a friend, because as Mike Whalen is prone to say....."Farming is everyone's bread and butter."®

III

Notes & Recipes

Table of Contents

Monthly Planting Tips 1-14

Appetizers and Beverages 15-24

Breads, Soups and Salads 25-52

Fish and Poultry 53-82

Beef and Pork 83-114

Desserts 115-130

Freezing and Canning 131-176

List Your Favorite Recipes

Recipes **Page**

MONTHLY PLANTING TIPS

January 1

February 2

March 3-4

April 5

May 6

June 7

July 8

August 9

September 10

October 11

November 12

December 13

List Your Favorite Recipes

Recipes   **Page**

January

Tips for care of your Christmas Gift Plants:

Poinsettias Flowering plants need average humidity. Let soil dry between waterings. Use water soluble fertilizer.

Amaryllis Bulb is usually semi-dormant when received--water, but don't soak. After growth is 6 inches tall, place in sunny location to bloom. Turn daily to keep stalk straight.

New seed catalogues will help you plan this year's garden. Ask yourself what you want from your garden, what seeds and plants will be available locally before you plan your order. Remember, most times and most plants may not be as gorgeous as the picture or descriptions.

To mulch your perennial flower beds, you might want to lop off the branches of your discarded Christmas tree. The branches protect the perennials from the cold, dry wind and encourage snow to deposit on the beds. Another plan is to place the tree in the backyard, anchoring it with a steel fence post, then decorating it as a food course for birds. Birdseed treats, lemon slices, orange slices, apple chunks and peanut butter covered crackers can attract a variety of birds to the yard.

Winter is also a good time to clean and sharpen your garden tools, if you did not get this done earlier. Remember, clear shiny metal surfaces rust easily, so wipe your sharpened tools with an oily rag to leave a protective film.

"There are two kinds of people, those who do the work and those who take the credit. Try to be in the first group; there is less competition there." --Indira Ghandi

Monthly Planting Tips

February

. Many gardeners prefer starting their own seeds because of the greater variety. If the gardener has time and facilities, seed starting is a rewarding activity.

Valentines Day to St. Patrick's Day is the recommended time for starting seeds for Region 5 (Midwest)

1. Growth medium -   Seed starter mix or your own favorite mix.
2. Moisture -   Soak strong seeds first, then drain.
3. Seeds -   Use fresh seed from new varieties, tried and true seed you can trust.
4. Warmth -   75° to 80° is ideal. If using a starting tray, furnish heat from below the tray.
5. Light -   You may use fluorescent lamps inside, or adjust protective glass, on a cold frame, outdoors on sunny days. (I use an old storm window, angled over seeds to direct the sunshine.) When seedlings appear, protect from too much direct sun on fragile plants.

If you have seeds from last year, you can make your own seed tapes. Cut paper towels about 1 inch wide and as long as needed. Put spots of glue on the strip at appropriate spacing. Place 2 seeds on each spot of glue. When dry, roll up and label and it's ready to plant. Make a shallow groove in the soil at the proper depth, and cover with soil. Thin growing plants by snipping less vigorous plants off at soil level. This method avoids spilled seed envelopes.

When planning your garden, maybe include an extra row of beans, or other produce, to share with the hungry in your area.

Watch forsythe for signs of breaking dormancy. You might want to cut some to bring inside to force blooming.

"If fifty million people say a foolish thing, it is still a foolish thing."
--Bertrand Russell

Monthly Planting Tips

March

Outdoors

Don't remove protective plant covers too soon. An extra week or two of protection can't hurt and may save your plants from late cold surprises.

Indoors

Containers for starting seeds should be sterilized (1/3 cup bleach in 1 gallon of water) is effective. Only sterile medium should be used for seed starting

After seeds have started to grow, excessive moisture, low temperatures and crowding may promote damping off. Consistent bottom heat is best with only enough moisture to dampen the medium. It is possible to apply a fungicide to the growing surface if the seedlings are not sensitive to it.

Flats, peat plugs or small cells should be ready for transplanting. When large enough, seedlings should be transplanted to individual pots or larger flats with more space for root growth. Plants should be thinned so only the strongest are left.

Recommended temperatures
for germination   70° to 75° daytime
                                    50° to 60° nighttime

Tomatoes, peppers, squash, eggplant and cucumber seedlings need 70° to 80° daytime temperatures.

As soon as frost is out of the ground, dig compost or fertilizer into the garden beds.

As soon as the ground can be worked early, lettuce and radishes can be planted

March is the time to prune summer and fall blooming clematis. They should be pruned to 12 inches from the ground for best growth and flowering.

Late in the month, early potatoes, onion seeds, sets of plants, peas, spinach, turnips, asparagus and rhubarb can be planted.

"Never try to teach a pig to sing. It wastes your time…and it annoys the pig."

Monthly Planting Tips   3

March
(continued)

When the weather warms and the seedlings grow stronger, they should be moved outdoors for hardening off, in a cold frame, in a tray in a sunny location; maybe brought back inside at night if temperatures cool.

Guiding dates for transplanting or the dates of the normal last killing frost may be obtained by calling your local County Cooperative Extension Service.

Relatively little trouble with insects include beets, chard, Chinese cabbage, chives, lettuce, leeks, onion, parsnips, peas, radishes, spinach and sweet potatoes.

Approximate Growth Times

cantaloupe	3 to 4 weeks
cucumber	4 weeks
head lettuce, leaf lettuce	3 to 5 weeks
Brussels sprouts	4 to 6 weeks
broccoli, cabbage, cauliflower, tomatoes	5 to 7 weeks
peppers	6 to 8 weeks
onion plants, parsley	8 weeks

Weather conditions at the time of transplant is more important then the number of weeks for maturity.

"Even when the experts all agree, they may well be mistaken."
--Bertrand Russell

Monthly Planting Tips

April

If it's time to break new ground for your garden, and you do not have a cultivator, just spade the ground 8 to 10 inches deep. Turning the turf over, green-side down, will bury growing turf and weeds and provide organic matter where it is needed.

Fruiting crops, tomatoes and peppers, need full sun. If full sun is at a premium in your yard, the following vegetables are suggested for growing in partial shade:

beans	cauliflower	peas
beets	celery	potatoes
broccoli	kale	pumpkins
Brussels sprouts	leeks	rhubarb
cabbage	parsley	summer squash

Light shade - chard, leaf lettuce, radish, spinach.

During the first 2 weeks of April, pre-emergent herbicide can be spread on your lawn to control weeds.

Cucumber, summer squash and melons can be started indoors for setting out next month. Start hardening off plants you have started indoors by setting them out in your cold frame. Cool season plants (radishes, cabbage, leaf lettuce, onion sets, peas and radishes) not already in the garden should be started soon.

Now is the time to check your perennials to see how they wintered, and which annuals you might want to fill in. It's helpful to know what you want and need before you go to the nursery for plants.

"I'm an old man and I've seen much trouble…but most of it never happened."   --Mark Twain

Monthly Planting Tips

May

Finally the time has arrived to plant our seeds and set out our plants!

Broccoli, Brussels sprouts may be planted now.

Early plantings of green beans and summer squash, a second planting of beets, lettuce, potato, radishes and spinach.

Main crops of tomatoes and pepper can be seeded early this month.

Thin planted seeds to prevent crowding.

Harvest early radishes, lettuce and green onions.

Replant radishes, carrots, beets and lettuce.

Plant first sweet corn.

Keep up with the weeds!

Maybe plant another variety of sweet corn.

Continue harvesting asparagus.

Check plants for insects or disease. Treat early.

If necessary, wrap stems of tomato plants with foil to stop cutworms.

Support tomato plants and prune out suckers on plants.

Plant another crop of beans.

"What we call poor, is someone who has no animals and no garden..." --Patrick Kagoda of Uganda

In the fall, toads burrow about 3 feet deep in loose soil, using horny projections on their hind feet; hibernate until spring. Toads are an effective, organic form of pest control and they actually LIKE to live around people's homes. I hope you'll make your garden inviting to toads. Once you see one, rub its tummy after swallowing a bug, you'll never go back to sprays.

Bees are essential for pollination of many garden plants. Tomatoes and beans may flower but without pollination they cannot bear fruit. In recent years beans have suffered from a variety of problems and their population has declined. To help attract whatever bees are in your area, plant flowers such as Borage and Monarda that are favorites with bees. After coming to your garden for these attractive flowers bees will stay to pollinate your vegetables and fruit.

Monthly Planting Tips

June

Whether you buy spring plants at a grocery store, supermarket, garden center or nursery, check them for obvious pests. Aphids, spider mites and white flies are possibilities. Even if no problems are seen, it may be wise to give the new arrivals a hard water spray, then set them by themselves for a day or two.

Cucumbers, peppers and tomatoes should be mulched to keep the ground cool and prevent moisture loss.

First strawberries, cabbage and broccoli can be harvested for use and the broccoli can be frozen.

Fall pumpkins can be planted.

Tomato plants may be staked and pruned.

Beans and summer squash may be planted.

Blanch cauliflower heads by tying the leaves up over the head, preventing sun discoloration.

Peas should be ready for harvest. When they have finished bearing, cut the stems off at the ground level and pull the vines. Leave the root nodules in place. They still have some value in the soil.

Mulch between rows and around plants to retain soil moisture.

When you harvest your cabbages, cut the heads so several rows of bottom leaves are left on the stem. The small cabbage heads that develop in the axils of these leaves have a mild, sweet flavor and provide a second harvest from plants already in your garden.

Flowers

Continue to mulch it away from trunks to prevent disease. Prune shrubs as they finish flowering.

Transplant or direct-sow tender annuals. Plant summer and fall-blooming bulbs.

Pinch mums.

"The person who removes a mountain begins by carrying away small stones." --Chinese Proverb

"The only place where success comes before work...is in the dictionary."   --Vidal Sassoon

Monthly Planting Tips

July

Finally summer heat has arrived and weed seeds are germinating everywhere. Frequent pulling or hoeing will keep them under control.

As your broccoli florets form, keep them picked so they don't develop flowers.

Successive plantings of green beans, beets, carrots, leaf lettuce and started plants of cabbage, broccoli and cauliflower plants should be made beginning July 10 through 20.

Beans, peppers and sweet corn can use a side dressing of 33-0-0 fertilizer. A rate of 1 pound per 100 feet of row is recommended by Cooperative Extension Service.

Be sure to deadhead your annual flowers for continued flowering.

Set out house plants for their summer contact with reality, beginning with shade and filtered sun.

Set your lawnmower to cut at 3 inches. The turf grasses roots can use the shade.

The midsummer insect crop is developing. Apply appropriate sprays and dusts as needed. Follow manufacturer's instructions carefully.

Add compost as a side dressing for tomatoes and peppers.

Water your container plantings. Sun and hot winds can dry them out.

Keep your bird baths clean and filled with water to encourage these insect eaters to stay nearby.

Task of the month: Watering. Assess if a plant needs water by sticking your fingers a few inches into the soil. Water deeply if it feels dry.

Keep new transplants well watered until established in the garden soil.

Keep up with harvest. Sow cool-season crops directly for fall harvest. Sow parsley, dill and basil in pots for winter use. Transplant last month's seedlings to the garden. Turn the compost.

Place a small bunch of aromatic herbs on the car floor. When trapped behind exhaust fumes, gently tread on the herbs, releasing perfume of mint, lavender or rosemary.

"The service we render to others is really the rent we pay for our room on this earth." -   --W. Grenfell

Monthly Planting Tips

August

It's time to plant for fall vegetable gardening. Lettuce, beans and radishes should be started in early August for late harvest around frost.

Drought stress is an invitation to disease and insect attack. Watering trees and shrubs deeply is the best prevention. Soil water loss can be minimized by mulching around the base of your plants.

If you use any form of tobacco, remember, most tobacco products have tobacco mosaid virus. It will not infect you, but you can spread it to your plants. Washing with soap and water will disinfect your hands.

Pick pears when they are still somewhat immature. They can ripen safely in a cool cellar.

Unless you need all of your tomatoes fully ripened, pick some while they are still pale green and pickle them whole. Pickle green tomatoes, well flavored with dill and garlic, are a real treat.

Since there is usually no shortage of zucchini, be imaginative in your use of them. Zucchini salsa, either medium or very hot, and zucchini bread are two of the best uses that can be made of this abundant crop.

Wash gourds before drying, to be sure they are free of soil and the garden debris. They may be dipped in a weak bleach solution of 1 part chlorine bleach to 10 parts water to sterilize the surface and prevent rotting. Hang gourds for drying in a warm location. After drying, the gourd's exterior can be polished with wax or coated with shellac. Dippers, bird houses and other containers should be pierced with a wire at the neck and hung until thoroughly dry.

Keep up with harvest. Collect herbs to freeze and dry. Begin harvesting dill, coriander and fennel seed.

"When one tugs at a single thing in nature, he finds it attached to the rest of the world.　　　　　　　　　　　　　　　　　--John Muir

Monthly Planting Tips

September

Pull plants that have finished bearing and add to the compost.
Cut or pull weeds to keep them from bearing seeds.
Pick grapes for eating, jam or wine.
Weed the strawberry patch. Apply a recommended herbicide.
Pick crabapples and apples as they ripen.
Sow winter onion seeds.
Pick herbs from drying or freezing.
Pick all broccoli heads that may be flowering, for continued production.
Dig iris and day lilies to separate and thin the plantings.
Check peach trees for gunny masses at ground level. These indicate borers and can be dug out with a sharp knife.
According to Dave Robson, University of Illinois Cooperative Extension Service Horticulture Educator, the 10 basic rules of gardening also apply to lawn care:
Rule #1 - Don't fight nature.
Rule #2 - 2-10 - see rule #1

Flowers

Continue to cut back leggy plants that are past their peak of bloom and divide crowded perennials. Remove any compost spent on frost-killed annuals. Keep pots of new plants well watered before and after planting. Take cuttings of coleus and geraniums to winter indoors. Plant early spring-flowering bulbs after soil temperature drops below 60°. Unearth and properly store summer bulbs.

Organic matter is the universal ingredient for a healthy productive soil. A green manure, a crop that is turned under before it goes to seed, is an economical means of adding organic matter. The decayed plant material adds humus to the soil.

Gardeners are the most optimistic people on earth,
Regardless of weather, diseases and insects,
Every spring they start again
with hearts full of hope, that this year
Their plants will grow to their expectation.

Monthly Planting Tips

October

Dig your sweet potatoes before a hard freeze and begin curing them for storage. Pick your last peppers and tomatoes before frost. They will keep stored in a cool place. Green tomatoes can be pickled just like cucumbers and they are delicious after a couple of months to absorb the dill and garlic. Harvest your squash and pumpkins but don't break off the stems. Cut them, leaving an inch or two attached to the vegetable.

Take slips of geraniums for drying and propagating indoors. You can also dig up whole plants, brush the soil off their roots and hang them in a cool dry place for replanting or slipping in spring.

Pick or buy your apples for winter storage. They should be at their peak quality now.

Check selected plants from which you want to save seeds. Then collect the seeds when they are mature and dry, but before they become scattered.

Don't cover the Brussels sprouts - their flavor is enhanced by a nip of frost.

October is normally our first frost month and the most probable date is from Columbus Day to mid-month.

If your house plants vacationed outdoors for the summer, it is time to bring them inside. Check for insects on plants and oil. If necessary, wash with a water spray or apply a people/pet friendly house plant insecticide.

Although late September through mid-October is best to ensure adequate time for root growth, bulbs can be plated until the ground freezes. Fall planted bulbs need a good soaking.

After frost, clean up garden areas and let the plants serve a second time by composting them. You may need to start an additional compost bin for the fall garden debris.

The rains that nourish the optimist's flowers also make the pessimist's weeds grow. --Anonymous

Monthly Planting Tips   11

November

Fall is the season when nature presents gardeners with a real resource--free for the taking. Some homeowners regard fall and fallen leaves as a reason for not having trees. Leaves of any kind are a benefit if used wisely.

Drain the crankcases of any 4-cycle engines and fill with clean oil. Be sure the fuel tanks are drained. Some experts recommend removing spark plugs from 2 or 4 cycle engines, squirting some clean engine oil into the cylinders, then replacing the plugs for over winter. This will keep an oily film on the upper cylinder walls to prevent rust damage.

Protect fruit trees and roses from rabbits with chicken wire and hardware cloth (over perennials and mulch after the ground is frozen).

Before temperatures reach 15°, mulch strawberry plants with 2 to 4 inches of straw.

Monthly Planting Tips

December

Don't worry if you saw some bulb foliage pop out of the ground this fall. Temperature and moisture levels can stimulate late growth. We may fear the plants won't bloom next spring, but they always do.

If you are a seed saver you can include a personal remembrance in the Christmas anniversary or birthday cards you send to gardener friends. An aluminum foil vacker, a coin envelope or a small plastic bag with seeds of a favorite flower or vegetable, enclosed in a card will make the occasion twice as memorable.

"Show me your garden and I shall tell you what you are."
--Alfred Austin (1835-1913)

"Knowing and not doing is the same as not knowing at all."
--Fortune Cookie

Really devoted gardeners, hearing Santa Claus say "Ho, Ho, Ho..." hear instead "Hoe, Hoe, Hoe" and think of spring.

Monthly Planting Tips

Notes & Recipes

14

Monthly Planting Tips

APPETIZERS

Appetizers

Beef Roll-Ups
Blue Cheese Ball
Caesar Salad Spread 15
Chicken Puffs
Chicken Salad
Cinnamon-Sugared Nuts 16
Cocktail Sauce Shrimp
Feta Cheese Dip
Fruit Dip
Fruit Dip 17
Fruit Dip
Georgia Caviar
Ham Roll-Ups 18
Hawaiian Bread Dip
Herbed Cheese Spread 19

Shrimp Dip
Smoked Salmon Dip
Stuffed Mild Jalapeños 20
Stuffed Mushrooms
Vegetable Dip 21

Beverages

Bloody Mary Mix 21
Frozen Strawberry Daiquiri
Jade Punch
Orange Blossom Punch 22
Orange Drink
Orange Punch
Slush Punch 23
Warm Citrus Drink 24

List Your Favorite Recipes

Recipes   **Page**

Beef Roll-Ups

1 pkg. chipped beef, sliced
2 (8 oz.) pkg. cream cheese
Horseradish, to taste

Sm. whole pickles, dill
is best, drained

CREAM horseradish and cream cheese until spreadable.
SEPARATE beef, spread one slice of beef with cheese mixture.
TOP with another slice of beef and another layer of cheese mixture.
PLACE pickle at edge and roll jellyroll-style.
REFRIGERATE until firm, slice in 1/2-inch slices and place tooth-
pick in center of pickle.
SERVE.

Blue Cheese Ball

3 to 5 oz. blue cheese
8 oz. cream cheese
1/4 tsp. garlic salt

1 T. pimento pepper
1 T. green pepper
Pecans, chopped

CHOP the peppers fine. Mix with the rest of ingredients.
ROLL into a ball.
CHILL until firm.
ROLL in chopped pecans.
SERVE with crackers.

Caesar Salad Spread

8 oz. Feta cheese
1 sm. can chopped black
  olives
1 tomato, chopped into
  sm. pieces

1 bunch green onions, chopped
  into sm. pieces
1/2 c. Caesar salad dressing

MIX above ingredients together and serve with crackers.

Appetizers

Chicken Puffs

1 c. water
1/2 c. margarine or butter
1 c. flour
4 eggs
6 dashes Tabasco sauce
1/4 c. grated Parmesan cheese

IN medium saucepan, combine margarine or butter, 1 cup water and 1/8 teaspoon salt.
BRING to a boil; add flour all at once, stirring vigorously.
COOK and stir until mixture forms a ball that doesn't separate. Remove from heat; cool 10 minutes.
ADD eggs, one at a time, beating with a wooden spoon after each addition, until smooth.
DROP batter by heaping tablespoons 3 inches apart onto a greased baking sheet.
BAKE in a 400° oven. Add Parmesan cheese before baking in oven for 30 to 35 minutes, or until golden.
COOL on wire rack.

Chicken Salad

2 chicken breasts, boiled,
   seasoned & diced
1 can sliced olives
2 celery ribs, chopped fine
2 green onions, chopped fine
1 c. mayonnaise

MIX together above ingredients until mayonnaise covers all, and refrigerate for 1 to 2 hours.
SPLIT puffs open for filling with chicken salad.
MAKES about 12 puffs, depending on size you make them.

Cinnamon-Sugared Nuts

1 beaten egg white
2 c. pecans
1/4 c. sugar
2 tsp. ground cinnamon
1/4 tsp. ground nutmeg
1/4 tsp. ground cloves

MIX pecan and egg whites to coat pecans.
ADD remaining ingredients and stir until completely coated.
SPREAD on cookie sheet in single layer and bake 25 to 30 minutes at 300°.

Appetizers

Cocktail Sauce Shrimp

1 lb. cooked, no-tails-on
    shrimp
1 bunch cilantro

1 T. olive oil
1 T. fresh chopped garlic
Cocktail sauce

IN large plastic bag, put all the ingredients, except cocktail sauce.
SHAKE well.

Feta Cheese Dip

8 oz. Feta cheese, crumbled
8 oz. Neufchatel cream cheese
2/3 c. mayonnaise
1/2 tsp. dill weed

1/2 tsp. dried basil
1/2 tsp. thyme
1/2 tsp. oregano
1 clove garlic

MIX with beater, cream cheese and mayonnaise.
ADD Feta cheese and garlic.
ADD spices and mix together.
CHILL.
SERVE with vegetables or crackers.

Fruit Dip

2 pkg. strawberry cream cheese
1/2 c. powdered sugar

1 lg. ctn. Cool Whip
1 (13 oz.) jar marshmallow creme

MIX cream cheese, sugar, Cool Whip and marshmallow creme together until smooth.
SERVE with bite-sized pieces of strawberries, peaches, apples and cantaloupe.

Fruit Dip

1 (8 oz.) pkg. cream cheese
1 sm. jar marshmallow creme

2 T. orange juice
1/4 c. powdered sugar

CREAM together first 3 ingredients.
FOLD in marshmallow creme.
SERVE as a dip with favorite fruit.

Appetizers

Fruit Dip

1 (8 oz.) pkg. cream cheese,
   softened
3/4 c. dark brown sugar

1/4 c. white sugar
1 T. vanilla

CREAM together with mixer until smooth.
REFRIGERATE until ready to serve.
SERVE with fresh fruits.

Georgia Caviar

3 cans black-eyed peas
1/2 c. jalapeño peppers,
   chopped
1 can tomatoes, chopped
   (no juice)
3/4 c. chopped onion

1 c. green pepper, chopped
1/4 c. pimento peppers,
   chopped
1 1/2 tsp. minced garlic
1 (8 oz.) btl. Italian dressing

MIX all ingredients; place in refrigerator and let flavors blend overnight.
SERVE with tortilla chips.

Ham Roll-Ups

5 lg. tortillas
2 (8 oz.) pkg. cream cheese
1/3 c. mayonnaise
1 sm. bunch green onions

1/4 c. black olives
1 (2 1/2 oz.) pkg. ham
1/8 tsp. garlic salt

MIX together cream cheese, mayonnaise, green onions, black olives and garlic salt.
SET in refrigerator for 10 minutes, then spread mixture on tortillas and place ham on top of mixture.
ROLL up tightly.
COVER and refrigerate overnight.
CUT off ends and cut each roll into thin slices.

Appetizers

Hawaiian Bread Dip

1 loaf round Hawaiian
    bread
1 1/2 c. sour cream
1 1/2 c. chopped ham
1 (8 oz.) pkg. cream
    cheese, softened

1/3 c. chopped onions
2 c. shredded Cheddar cheese
1/3 c. chopped chilies
Dash of Worcestershire sauce

SLICE off top of bread and hollow out.
MIX all ingredients and put inside bread.
WRAP in foil.
BAKE at 350° for 1 hour.
USE pieces of bread and crackers as dippers.

Herbed Cheese Spread

4 oz. cream cheese,
    softened
1/3 c. sour cream
2 c. shredded Colby/Jack
    cheese

2 T. parsley
2 T. green onions, finely
    chopped
1/2 tsp. paprika
1/4 tsp. hot pepper sauce

BEAT cream cheese and sour cream until well blended.
STIR in remaining ingredients; mix well.
SPOON into container.
REFRIGERATE.
MAKES 2 cups.
SERVE at any time with your favorite cracker.

Appetizers

Shrimp Dip

1 can shrimp
1 bunch green onions
1 jar shrimp sauce
1 (8 oz.) pkg. cream cheese

1 can black olives
1 (8 oz.) pkg. Mozzarella
   cheese
1 round aluminum pan

SPREAD softened cream cheese on pan.
POUR shrimp sauce over cream cheese.
SPRINKLE can of shrimp over shrimp sauce.
SPRINKLE Mozzarella cheese on top of shrimp.
CUT onion and black olives and sprinkle on top of cheese.
CUT for 1 hour and serve with crackers.

Smoked Salmon Dip

1 1/2 lb. smoked salmon
   or 2 cans
2 c. thousand island dressing
2 tsp. dried onion

2 tsp. celery salt
1/2 tsp. garlic powder
3 T. Worcestershire sauce
2 T. liquid smoke

FLAKE fish; mix all ingredients together and chill.
SERVE with crackers of choice.

Stuffed Mild Jalapeños

8 oz. Hellmann's mayonnaise
12 oz. bacon, cooked crisp
   & crumbled
2 sm. bunches green onion,
   chopped

8 oz. sharp Cheddar cheese,
   grated
10 oz. chopped pecans or
   almonds
1 (12 oz.) cans mild jalapeño
   pepper halves

DRAIN jalapeños; rinse and pat dry.
MIX all remaining ingredients.
STUFF jalapeños.
REFRIGERATE.

Appetizers

Stuffed Mushrooms

Fresh mushroom caps
Italian sausage
Chopped green pepper
Chopped onions
Monterey Jack cheese

TAKE off stems of mushrooms; clean.
MIX fresh Italian sausage with remaining ingredients.
STUFF inside mushroom caps.
BAKE for about 20 minutes; add Monterey Jack cheese on top.
SERVE.

Vegetable Dip

2 eggs, slightly beaten
2 T. sugar
2 T. vinegar
1 1/2 T. butter
6 oz. cream cheese
1/2 mild onion, minced
1/2 green pepper, minced

COOK eggs, sugar, vinegar and butter over medium heat, stirring constantly until thickened; let cool.
SOFTEN and beat cream cheese until fluffy.
ADD to cooled mixture along with onion and green pepper.
BEST made a day ahead to allow to cool.

Bloody Mary Mix

1 (No. 5) can tomato juice
3/4 c. beef consommé
1/2 tsp. Tabasco sauce
1/2 tsp. lemon juice
1 1/2 tsp. Worcestershire sauce
1 tsp. celery salt
1 tsp. salt
1/2 tsp. pepper

COMBINE all ingredients and mix well. Store, covered, under refrigeration. Mix well. Will keep several days.
MAKES 1 1/2 quarts.
TO PREPARE drink: Fill glass with ice and pour in 1 ounce vodka, may also make without vodka.
ADD Bloody Mary Mix, stir slightly to blend.
GARNISH with a lime wedge and/or celery stick.

Appetizers

Frozen Strawberry Daiquiri

1 (6 oz.) can limeade or
    lemonade concentrate,
    thawed
2 T. sugar

12 1/2 oz. light rum
3 c. cracked ice
25 lg. fresh frozen strawberries

BLEND lemonade or limeade, strawberries, sugar, rum and cracked ice for 30 seconds.
POUR into 1 1/2 to 3 pitchers half-filled with ice cubes.
YIELD: 8 to 12 servings.

Jade Punch

1 sm. pkg. lime Jello
1 c. pineapple juice
1 (28 oz.) btl. ginger ale

1 (6 oz.) can frozen lemonade,
    undiluted
Whole fresh strawberries (opt.)

DISSOLVE lime Jello in 1 cup hot water.
ADD 2 cups cold water, pineapple juice and frozen lemonade. Blend well.
JUST before serving, add the ginger ale, ice cubes and fresh strawberries.

Orange Blossom Punch

1 c. frozen orange juice
    concentrate, thawed
1 (10 oz.) can frozen
    strawberry or peach
    daiquiri mix concentrate,
    thawed

1 (750 ml) btl. champagne or
    sparkling white grape juice,
    chilled
Ice cubes

IN a punch bowl, combine thawed concentrates.
ADD 4 cups cold water; stir to combine.
GENTLY add champagne or grape juice, but do not stir.
SERVE immediately over ice.
IF desired, garnish with strawberries and orange wedges.
MAKES 12 servings.

Beverages

Orange Drink

1 qt. reconstituted orange
    juice

1 pkg. noninstant vanilla
    pudding & pie filling
1 env. Dream Whip

IN blender, pour orange juice and 1 package noninstant vanilla
pudding and pie filling, and blend a "second".
ADD 1 envelope Dream Whip and blend a "second".
SERVE - delicious.

Orange Punch

1 can orange Hi-C
2 sm. cans frozen lemonade
1 lg. can pineapple juice

1 btl. ginger ale
1 pkg. orange Kool-Aid mixed
    with water

MIX well and chill.
MAKES 2 gallons.

Slush Punch

2 pkg. Kool-Aid (and flavor)
3 qt. water
1 (6 oz.) can frozen
    lemonade

2 c. sugar
1 (6 oz.) can frozen orange
    juice
1 qt. ginger ale

COMBINE all ingredients until dissolved.
FREEZE, stir occasionally.
WHEN ready to serve, add ginger ale.

Beverages

Warm Citrus Drink

3 c. orange juice
1 c. grapefruit juice

1/4 c. honey
1 (3") piece of cinnamon stick

IN medium saucepan, combine orange juice, grapefruit juice, honey and cinnamon.
HEAT, stirring occasionally, just until warm (do not boil).
REMOVE cinnamon with slotted spoon; discard.
SERVE warm. If desired, garnish with orange slices.
MAKES 4 or 5 servings.

Beverages

BREADS, SOUPS AND SALADS

Breads

Great Picnic Rolls
Green Onion French Bread 25
Herb Bread
Sweet Potato Bread 26
Tortillas 27
Vegetable Bread 28

Soups

Beer-Cheese Soup 28
Bell Pepper-Cheese Chowder
Borscht 29
Cold Cucumber Soup
Cream of Zucchini Soup 30
Creamy Asparagus-and-
    Chicken Soup 31
Creamy Spinach Soup
Creme Vichyssoise 32
Double-Cheese French Onion
    Soup
Fruit Soup 33
Garden Chowder
Gazpacho 34
Green Chile Soup In a
    Crock-Pot
Icy Olive Soup 35
Macaroni and Cheese Soup
Ruby-Red Rhubarb Soup 36
Strawberry Soup
Summer Garden Vegetable
    Soup 37
Sweet Potato and Sausage
    Soup 38

Salads

American French Dressing 38
Apple Salad
Broccoli Salad 39
Cabbage Crock Salad
Cabbage Salad Dressing
Cauliflower with Parmesan and
    Bacon 40
Chicken Caesar Salad
Cold Chicken 41
Cooked Mayonnaise
Cottage Cheese Fruit Salad
Deviled Eggs 42
Deviled Eggs
Dilly Marinated Vegetable
    Salad
Fiesta Salad 43
Fire and Ice Tomatoes
Freezer Coleslaw 44
Frozen Fruit Salad
Fruit Salad Dressing 45
Garlic and Herb Dressing
Golden Dressing 46
Hot Potato Salad
Macaroni Salad 47
Macaroni-Tuna Salad
Mushroom-Stuffed Tomatoes ... 48
Liberty Red, White and Blue
    Salad 49
Marinated Potato Salad 50
Pasta-Vegetable Salad 51
Pickled Carrots
Sweet-Sour Cucumbers
Taffy Apple Salad 52

List Your Favorite Recipes

Recipes **Page**

Great Picnic Rolls

1 pkg. vanilla pudding mix	1/2 c. warm water
1 stick butter or margarine	2 eggs
2 pkg. yeast	1 tsp. salt
2 tsp. sugar	5 1/2 to 6 c. flour

COOK pudding as directed on package. Add 1 stick of margarin
butter. Cool to lukewarm.
MIX yeast and sugar in warm water. Add to lukewarm pudd
mixture.
ADD eggs, salt and flour.
KNEAD until mixed.
LET rise until doubled.
SHAPE into rolls.
LET rise again.
BAKE at 350° until light brown, about 20 minutes.

Green Onion French Bread

3/4 c. (3 oz.) shredded	1/4 c. green onions
Cheddar cheese	1/4 tsp. pepper
1/2 c. mayonnaise	1 (16 oz.) loaf unsliced French
1/4 c. butter or margarine,	bread
softened	

COMBINE first 5 ingredients, stirring well. Slice bread in half
lengthwise. Spread cheese mixture on cut sides of bread.
PLACE bread on an ungreased baking sheet; broil 5 1/2 inches from
heat (with electric oven door partially opened), 3 minutes, or until
cheese topping is bubbly.
YIELD: 1 loaf.

Breads

Herb Bread

3/4 c. milk
2 T. bacon fat or oil
2 T. sugar
1/2 tsp. salt
1 pkg. yeast
1/4 c. water

1 egg
1/4 c. chopped chives
2 T. parsley
1 tsp. oregano
3 to 3 1/2 c. flour

HEAT first 4 ingredients.
COOL.
MIX yeast and water.
ADD liquid, eggs and herbs to yeast.
STIR in 2 cups flour.
ADD rest of flour.
KNEAD.
LET rise until double.
SHAPE in round loaf in 9-inch pie pan.
LET rise again, about 30 minutes.
BAKE at 400° for 10 minutes, and at 375° for 20 minutes.

Sweet Potato Bread

1/4 c. butter or margarine
1/2 c. packed brown sugar
2 eggs
1 c. mashed sweet potatoes
3 T. milk
1 tsp. grated orange peel

2 c. self-rising flour (may use
2 c all-purpose flour, 1 T.
baking powder & 1 tsp. salt)
1/4 tsp. ground allspice
1/4 tsp. ground nutmeg
2 T. chopped pecans

IN a mixing bowl, cream butter or margarine and brown sugar.
ADD eggs; mix well. Add sweet potatoes, milk and orange peel; mix well.
COMBINE flour, allspice and nutmeg.
ADD to creamed mixture; mix just until combined. Fold in nuts.
POUR into a 9x5x3-inch loaf pan coated with nonstick cooking spray.
BAKE at 350° for 40 to 45 minutes, or until bread tests done.
COOL in pan for 10 minutes before removing to a wire rack; cool
completely.

ORANGE CREAM SPREAD:
3 oz. cream cheese, softened

1 tsp. orange juice
1 tsp. grated orange peel

COMBINE ingredients; beat until smooth. Serve with bread.

Breads

Tortillas

3 1/2 c. all-purpose flour
1 tsp. salt
3/4 tsp. baking powder

1/3 c. shortening
1 c. warm water (105° to 115°)

COMBINE first 3 ingredients; stir well.
CUT in shortening with pastry blender until mixture resembles coarse meal.
STIR in milk, mixing well.
TURN dough out onto a smooth surface; knead about 3 minutes.
DIVIDE dough into 10 equal portions.
ROLL each with a rolling pin into a very thin circle, about 8 inches in diameter, turning dough and rolling on both sides.
HEAT on ungreased skillet over medium heat; cook tortillas about 2 minutes on each side, or until lightly browned, being careful not to let tortillas wrinkle.
PAT tortillas lightly with spatula while browning the second side.
SERVE hot.
YIELD: 10 tortillas.

Making your own tortillas really makes all your recipes so much better. You will find so many more ways to use them when you make them yourself. Many stores now carry tortilla presses, but it is not difficult to roll your own.
With such a busy lifestyle, we all experience during the summer months, you will find tortillas will come in so handy for unique recipes from breakfast through late-night snacks.

Breads

Vegetable Bread

These are great with breakfasts

3 (10 oz.) cans refrigerator
    buttermilk biscuits
1/2 c. butter or margarine, melted
1/2 lb. bacon, cooked & crumbled

1/2 c. grated Parmesan cheese
1 sm. onion, finely chopped
1 sm. green pepper, finely
    chopped

CUT biscuits into quarters; dip each piece in butter and layer 1/3 in a lightly-greased 10-inch bundt pan.
SPRINKLE with half each of bacon, cheese, onion and green pepper.
REPEAT layers until all ingredients are used, ending with biscuits.
BAKE at 350° for 40 to 45 minutes, or until done.
YIELD: 1 (10-inch) ring.

Beer-Cheese Soup

3 c. milk
1 (12 oz.) can beer
1 (16 oz.) pkg. processed
    cheese spread, cubed
1 1/2 tsp. chicken-flavored
    bouillon granules

3 dashes hot sauce
1/4 c. + 2 T. all-purpose
    flour
1/4 c. water

COMBINE milk and beer in a Dutch oven.
COOK over low heat until thoroughly heated, stirring frequently.
ADD cheese spread, bouillon granules and hot sauce.
COOK on low heat until thoroughly heated, stirring constantly (do not boil).
YIELD: 6 cups.

MICROWAVE DIRECTIONS:
COMBINE milk and beer in a 3-quart casserole.
MICROWAVE at HIGH for 4 to 5 minutes.
ADD cheese spread, bouillon granules and hot sauce.
STIR well with a wire whisk.
MICROWAVE at HIGH for 5 to 6 minutes, or until cheese melts, stirring every 2 minutes.
COMBINE flour and water, stirring until smooth.
GRADUALLY stir in flour mixture; microwave at HIGH for 4 to 5 minutes, or until thickened, stirring every minute.

Soups

Bell Pepper-Cheese Chowder

2 T. margarine
1 c. chopped red bell pepper
1 c. chopped yellow
   bell pepper
1/2 c. chopped carrots
1/2 c. celery
1/2 c. chopped onion
2 cloves garlic, minced
3/4 c. all-purpose flour
3 c. milk
2 1/2 c. canned chicken broth

1/2 tsp. dry mustard
1/4 tsp. dried rosemary,
   crushed
1/4 tsp. salt
1/4 tsp. red pepper
1/2 tsp. ground black pepper
1 1/2 c. (6 oz.) Cheddar cheese
1 1/2 c. flat light beer
Garnish with fresh rosemary
   sprigs

MELT margarine in a large Dutch oven over medium-high heat. Add red bell pepper and next 5 ingredients; cook, stirring constantly, 5 minutes, or until tender.
COMBINE flour, milk and chicken broth, stirring until smooth. Gradually stir into vegetable mixture; cook, stirring constantly, until thick and bubbly.
STIR in mustard and next 4 ingredients; gradually add cheese and beer, stirring until cheese melts. Garnish if desired, and serve immediately.
YIELD: 10 cups.

Borscht

1 (16 oz.) can whole
   beets, undrained
1 (10 3/4 oz.) can chicken
   broth, undiluted

1 (8 oz.) ctn. sour cream
1/8 tsp. white pepper
1 1/2 tsp. lemon juice
2 T. chopped chives

COMBINE beets and broth in container of an electric blender or food processor.
PROCESS until smooth.
COMBINE beet purée, sour cream, pepper and lemon juice; stir well.
CHILL.
SPRINKLE each serving of soup with chives.
SERVES: 4.

Soups

Cold Cucumber Soup

1 1/2 c. sour cream
1/2 tsp. dried whole dill
1 T. Worcestershire sauce
2 green onions, coarsely
   chopped

3 med. cucumbers, peeled,
   seeded & coarsely chopped
1/2 tsp. celery salt
1 T. lemon juice
1/4 tsp. pepper

COMBINE all ingredients in an electric blender; process until smooth.
CHILL thoroughly.
YIELD: 3 1/2 cups.

Cream of Zucchini Soup

2 c. sliced zucchini
1/2 c. chopped onion
1/2 c. chopped carrot
1 T. butter or margarine
2 c. chicken broth

3/4 c. dried tarragon
1/2 tsp. salt
1/4 tsp. pepper
1/4 to 1/2 tsp. garlic powder
2 c. milk

IN a large saucepan over medium heat, sauté zucchini, onion and carrot in butter for 5 minutes. Add broth, tarragon, salt, pepper and garlic powder; bring to a boil.
REDUCE heat; cover and simmer for 15 to 20 minutes, or until vegetables are tender. Purée in a blender or food processor; return to pan. Add milk; heat through.
YIELD: 4 servings.

Soups

Creamy Asparagus-and-Chicken Soup

4 (4 oz.) skinned & boned
   chicken breast halves
4 c. water
1 med. onion, quartered
2 lg. celery stalks, cut
   into 1" pieces
1 tsp. salt

1/2 tsp. pepper
1 1/2 lb. fresh asparagus
1 c. nonfat sour cream (may
   use regular sour cream)
1 c. milk (may use skim)
Chopped fresh parsley,
   for garnish

COMBINE first 6 ingredients in a saucepan; bring to a boil. Cover and reduce heat; simmer 35 minutes, or until chicken is tender.

REMOVE chicken, reserving broth and vegetables in pan. let chicken cool slightly; shred into bite-size pieces and set aside.

SNAP off tough ends of asparagus; remove scales from stalks with a vegetable peeler, if desired. Cut asparagus into 2-inch pieces; add to reserved chicken broth and vegetables.

BRING to a boil; cover and reduce heat. Simmer 10 minutes or until asparagus is tender. Drain vegetable mixture, reserving broth in pan.

POSITION knife blade in food processor bowl; add vegetables and 1 cup reserved broth. Process until smooth, scrape down sides once. Add sour cream; process until smooth.

GRADUALLY add purée to remaining broth in pan; stir in milk and chicken. Cook over low heat (do not boil), serve warm.

Soups

Creamy Spinach Soup

1 lg. onion, diced
3 T. butter or margarine,
   melted
1 med. potato, cut into
   quarters
1/4 c. cooked, diced ham
2 beef-flavored bouillon
   cubes
1/4 tsp. salt
1/4 tsp. pepper

1/8 tsp. ground nutmeg
1 clove garlic, minced
1 c. water
1 (10 oz.) pkg. frozen, drained,
   or 1 lb. fresh spinach,
   cooked & drained
3 1/2 c. half & half or milk
Croutons (opt.)
Grated Parmesan cheese
   (opt.)

SAUTÉ onion in butter in large Dutch oven. Add next 8 ingredients. Bring to a boil; cover and reduce heat. Simmer 15 to 20 minutes, or until potato is tender, stirring occasionally.
COMBINE potato mixture and spinach in container of an electric blender; process until smooth.
RETURN mixture to Dutch oven; stir in half & half.
COOK over low heat, stirring constantly, until heated.
GARNISH each serving with croutons, and sprinkle with cheese, if desired.
YIELD: 6 cups.

Creme Vichyssoise

2 c. coarsely-chopped leeks
   with tops, or onions
3 c. peeled, sliced potatoes
3 c. water
4 chicken-flavored bouillon
   cubes

1/4 tsp. white pepper
3 T. butter or margarine
2 c. half & half or milk
2 T. chopped chives

COMBINE first 6 ingredients in a Dutch oven; cook over medium heat until vegetables are tender.
PURÉE in an electric blender.
STIR in half & half, and chill.
GARNISH with chives.
YIELD: 6 1/2 cups.

Soups

Double-Cheese French Onion Soup

4 lg. onions, thinly sliced
   & separated into rings
1/2 c. butter or margarine,
   melted
1 T. all-purpose flour
1 (10 3/4 oz.) can chicken
   broth, undiluted
1 (10 1/2 oz.) can beef
   broth, undiluted

2 c. water
1/4 c. dry white wine
1/8 to 1/4 tsp. pepper
8 (3/4" thick) slices of
   French bread, toasted
8 slices Mozzarella cheese
1/2 c. grated Parmesan cheese

SAUTÉ onion in butter in a Dutch oven until tender.
BLEND in flour, stirring until smooth.
GRADUALLY add chicken broth, beef broth, water and wine.
BRING to a boil; reduce heat and simmer 15 minutes. Add pepper.
PLACE 8 oven-proof serving bowls on a baking sheet.
PLACE 1 bread slice in each bowl; ladle soup over bread.
TOP with 1 cheese slice; sprinkle with Parmesan cheese.
BROIL 6 inches from heat until cheese melts.
YIELD: 8 cups.

Fruit Soup

1 (12 oz.) pkg. pitted prunes
1 (6 oz.) pkg. dried apricots
1 (16 oz.) can sliced peaches
   in syrup
1 (8 oz.) pkg. pearl tapioca

1 (15 oz.) pkg. seedless white
   raisins
6 apples, peeled, cored &
   sliced
Sugar

SOAK pearl tapioca overnight in water to cover.
COOK apples in water to cover until done, but still holding their
shape.
HEAT other ingredients except tapioca, separately in water.
COMBINE all ingredients (including liquid) in a large kettle.
ADD sugar to taste, and heat to dissolve sugar and cook tapioca.
REMOVE from heat; cool and serve chilled.

Soups

Garden Chowder

1/4 c. chopped onion
1/2 c. chopped celery
1/4 c. butter or margarine
1/4 c. all-purpose flour
1/2 tsp. salt
1/4 tsp. pepper
2 c. chicken broth

1 med. tomato, peeled &
   diced
1 c. broccoli florets
1 c. chopped carrots
1 c. frozen corn
1 c. thinly-sliced zucchini
2 c. half & half cream
1/4 c. Parmesan cheese

IN a 3-quart saucepan over medium heat, sauté onion and celery in
butter for 5 minutes. Add flour, salt and pepper; stir to form a smooth
paste. Gradually add broth, stirring constantly.
BRING to a boil; boil and stir for 2 minutes, or until thickened. Add
tomato, broccoli, carrots, corn and zucchini; return to a boil. Reduce
heat; cover and simmer for 40 minutes, or until vegetables are tender.
ADD cream and cheese; heat through.
YIELD: 4 to 6 servings.

Gazpacho

1 (10 1/2 oz.) can tomato
   soup, undiluted
1 1/2 c. tomato juice
1 1/4 c. water
1/2 to 1 c. chopped cucumber
1/2 to 1 c. chopped tomatoes
1/2 c. chopped green pepper
1/2 c. chopped onion

2 T. wine vinegar
1 T. commercial Italian
   dressing
1 T. lemon or lime juice
1 clove garlic, minced
1/4 tsp. pepper
1/4 tsp. hot sauce

COMBINE all ingredients; chill at least 6 hours.
YIELD: 6 cups.

Soups

Green Chile Soup In a Crock-Pot

1 1/2 lb. skinned & boned
   chicken breast halves,
   cut into 1" cubes
3 (4.5 oz.) cans chopped
   green chilies, undrained
1 (15 oz.) can pinto beans,
   undrained

1 (14 1/2 oz.) can stewed
   tomatoes, undrained
2 c. water
1 tsp. salt
1/4 tsp. ground cumin
1/4 tsp. dried oregano
1 lg. onion, chopped
1 clove garlic, crushed

TOPPINGS:
Sour cream
Shredded Cheddar cheese

Chopped avocado
Sliced green onions

PLACE first 10 ingredients in a 3 1/2 or 4-quart electric slow cooker.
COVER and cook on high 4 to 6 hours, or on low 8 hours.
SERVE soup with desired toppings.
YIELD 10 cups.

Icy Olive Soup

2 c. (16 oz.) plain yogurt
2 (10 1/2 oz. each) cans
   condensed chicken
   broth, undiluted
2 (2 1/4 oz. each) cans
   sliced ripe olives, drained

1 c. coarsely-chopped
   cucumber
1/2 c. chopped green onion
1/2 c. chopped green pepper
1/2 c. sliced stuffed olives
1/8 tsp. white pepper
Seasoned croutons (opt.)

IN a large bowl, stir yogurt until smooth. Whisk in broth.
ADD next 6 ingredients; mix well.
COVER and chill for 4 hours.
STIR before serving.
GARNISH with croutons, if desired.
YIELD: 6 servings.

Soups

Macaroni and Cheese Soup

3 qt. water
5 tsp. chicken bouillon granules
1 1/2 c. sliced celery
2 lg. carrots, shredded
1 lg. onion, chopped
1 med. green pepper, chopped

2 1/2 c. uncooked elbow macaroni
1 c. butter or margarine
3/4 c. all-purpose flour
6 c. milk
1 lb. processed American
   cheese, cubed

IN a soup kettle or Dutch oven, bring water and bouillon to a boil. Add celery, carrots, onion and green pepper; cook for 4 minutes, or until tender. Add macaroni. Cover and return to a boil; boil for 2 minutes. Remove from heat; let stand for 8 to 10 minutes, or until macaroni is just tender.
MEANWHILE, melt butter in saucepan. Add flour, stirring until smooth. Gradually add milk, stirring constantly. Bring to a boil; cook and stir for 2 minutes. Stir in cheese until melted; add to undrained macaroni mixture.
YIELD: 20 servings (5 quarts).

Ruby-Red Rhubarb Soup

4 c. sliced fresh or frozen
   rhubarb
1 qt. + 1 T. water, divided
2/3 c. sugar
1 T. cornstarch

1/2 tsp. red food coloring
   (opt.)
1 egg yolk, beaten
1/2 c. whipping cream

IN a 2-quart saucepan, combine rhubarb, 1 quart of water and sugar; bring to a boil. Reduce heat; cover and simmer for 20 minutes, or until rhubarb is tender.
COOL for 15 minutes. Place in a blender; process until smooth. Return to a pan.
DISSOLVE cornstarch in remaining water; stir into rhubarb mixture. Bring to a boil; boil for 2 minutes, stirring constantly. Add food coloring if desired; mix well.
ADD a small amount of soup to egg yolk, stirring constantly; return to pan.
CHILL.
JUST before serving, beat cream until very soft peaks form; fold into soup.
YIELD: 6 servings.

Strawberry Soup

2 qt. fresh strawberries,
  divided
1/2 c. water
5 T. sugar
1 T. all-purpose flour

1 tsp. grated orange peel
1 c. whipping cream
Fresh mint & additional
  strawberries (opt.)

MASH half the strawberries with a potato masher or fork; set aside.
IN blender, combine remaining strawberries, water, sugar, flour and
orange peel; process until smooth.
POUR into a 2-quart saucepan. Bring to a boil over medium heat; boil
for 2 minutes, stirring constantly.
ADD mashed strawberries. Reduce heat; simmer, uncovered, for 10
minutes, stirring constantly.
CHILL for at least 1 hour. Stir in cream.
COVER and chill overnight.
GARNISH with mint and strawberries, if desired.
YIELD: 4 servings.

Summer Garden Vegetable Soup

1 sm. head cabbage,
  chopped
2 med. sweet red peppers,
  chopped
6 med. tomatoes, peeled,
  seeded & chopped
1 T. parsley, chopped
1/4 tsp. garlic powder

3 med. green peppers, chopped
5 med. onions, chopped
3 celery ribs, chopped
4 c. chicken broth
1 bay leaf
1/4 tsp. dried thyme
Salt & pepper, to taste

COMBINE all ingredients in a large kettle or Dutch oven; bring to a
boil. Reduce heat.
COVER and simmer for 2 to 2 1/2 hours, or until vegetables are
tender, stirring occasionally.
REMOVE bay leaf before serving.

Soups

Sweet Potato and Sausage Soup

1/2 lb. smoked sausage, cut
    into 1/2" slices
1 med.-size sweet potato,
    peeled & cut into 1/2"
    cubes
1 c. coarsely-shredded
    cabbage
1/2 c. chopped bell pepper
1/2 c. chopped celery

1/2 c. chopped onion
8 fresh tomatoes, peeled &
    chopped
1 (15.8 oz.) can peas,
    undrained, or 1 to 2 c.
    fresh peas
1 (14 1/4 oz.) can beef broth
1/4 tsp. hot sauce

COMBINE all ingredients in a large Dutch oven; bring to a boil over
medium-high heat. Cover, reduce heat and simmer 30 minutes, or
until potato is tender, stirring occasionally.
YIELD: 7 cups.

American French Dressing

1/4 c. sugar
1 tsp. dry mustard
1 can condensed tomato
    soup, undiluted
1/2 c. cider vinegar

1 tsp. salt
1 T. paprika
1 c. salad oil
1 tsp. Worcestershire sauce

COMBINE ingredients in order listed.
MIX well by shaking in quart jar.
STORE in refrigerator; will not separate.

Salads

Apple Salad

2 eggs
5 T. lemon juice
5 T. sugar
5 T. butter
1/2 bag marshmallows
1/2 pt. whipping cream
2 red apples, cut up

2 yellow apples, cut up
2 bananas, cut up
1 c. grapes, cut in half
Pineapple tidbits
Maraschino cherries
Nuts

CREAM together sugar and eggs.
ADD lemon juice and butter.
COOK until thick.
REMOVE from heat and add marshmallows.
COOL well.
MIX with whipping cream.
POUR over fruit and nuts which have been placed in bowl.

Broccoli Salad

1 c. mayonnaise
Scant 1/2 c. sugar
3 T. red wine vinegar
4 c. broccoli (may also add
    2 c. cauliflower)

1/2 c. raisins
1/2 c. red onions, chopped
8 slices bacon, cooked,
    drained well & chopped

MIX together mayonnaise, sugar and vinegar; set aside.
MIX in remaining ingredients and add mayonnaise mixture; chill
about 2 hours, or more, to blend flavors.

Salads

Cabbage Crock Salad

1 lg. head cabbage	2 c. sugar
2 or 3 onions	2 c. cider vinegar
2 green peppers	1 T. celery seed
2 carrots	1 1/2 T. mustard seed
Salt water	

SHRED or chop vegetables and let soak several hours in salt water, using 1 tablespoon salt to a quart of water.
DRAIN, press out as much liquid as possible and dry with a towel.
HEAT sugar, vinegar, celery seed and mustard seed until sugar is dissolved.
LET cool, then mix with vegetables and chill well.

This salad is ready to eat as soon as cold, but will remain crisp and fresh in the refrigerator a long time. Store, covered, in a crock or a glass container.

Cabbage Salad Dressing

1 1/2 c. sugar	3 T. onion juice or grated onion
2 tsp. dry mustard	2 c. salad oil
2 tsp. salt	3 T. poppy seed (opt.)
2/3 c. vinegar	

Cauliflower with Parmesan and Bacon

1 sm. head iceberg lettuce, torn (8 c.)	1 T. sugar
	1/2 tsp. dried thyme, crushed
1/2 head cauliflower, coarsely chopped (3 c.)	1/2 c. grated Parmesan cheese
	1/2 lb. bacon, cooked & crumbled
1 purple onion, chopped	
1 c. mayonnaise or salad dressing	

LAYER first 3 ingredients in a large glass bowl.
COMBINE mayonnaise, sugar and thyme, stirring well; spoon mayonnaise mixture over vegetables, and sprinkle evenly with grated Parmesan cheese. Cover and chill 3 to 4 hours.
SPRINKLE with crumbled bacon just before serving.
YIELD: 6 to 8 servings.

Salads

Chicken Caesar Salad

4 skinned & boned chicken
   halves
1 1/2 tsp. lemon-pepper
   seasonings
1/4 c. olive oil
2 T. white wine vinegar

1 tsp. Dijon mustard
1/2 tsp. Worcestershire sauce
1 head romaine lettuce, torn
1 c. garlic croutons
1/4 c. Parmesan cheese

CUT chicken into 1/4-inch strips; sprinkle with lemon-pepper seasoning and garlic powder.

POUR olive oil into a large skillet, and place over medium-high heat until hot. Add chicken strips, and cook 4 to 5 minutes, or until done. Remove chicken strips and drain on paper towels, reserving drippings in skillet.

COMBINE vinegar, mustard and Worcestershire sauce; add to reserved drippings. Cook over medium heat, stirring until blended. Pour over romaine lettuce; add chicken and toss gently. Sprinkle with croutons and cheese; serve immediately.

YIELD: 4 servings.

Cold Chicken

1 whole chicken

MARINADE:
3 T. salad oil
6 T. sweet pickle juice
1 tsp. salt

6 T. lemon juice
1/2 tsp. onion juice
1/2 tsp. celery seed

STARTING the night before, boil chicken and cool. Bone and cut into chunks.

COMBINE marinade ingredients and add chicken chunks.

PLACE in container with tight seal and marinate overnight in the refrigerator.

NEXT day, mix in desired amount of mayonnaise and chill.

SERVE on lettuce leaf with croissants.

Salads

Cooked Mayonnaise

5 eggs
1 c. sugar
3 T. flour
1/4 tsp. dry mustard

1/4 tsp. salt
1/2 c. vinegar
1 c. water

BEAT eggs well.
MIX all ingredients well.
BRING to a boil, stirring constantly.
WHEN thickened, remove from heat.
REFRIGERATE.

Cottage Cheese Fruit Salad

1 sm. box red Jello (dry)
1 sm. ctn. cottage cheese,
  small curd
1 can pineapple tidbits,
  drained

1 can dark sweet cherries,
  drained
1 sm. ctn. Cool Whip
1/2 c. nuts (opt.)
1/2 c. coconut (opt.)

MIX Jello and cottage cheese.
ADD coconut and nuts, if desired.
NOTE: Other combinations to above salad, such as: orange Jello, pineapple and mandarin oranges; lime Jello, pineapple and sliced green seedless grapes; wild cherry Jello, dark cherries, mandarin oranges and marshmallows.

Deviled Eggs

1 doz. eggs
1 tsp. mustard
2 T. mayonnaise

4 T. pickle relish
Salt, to taste
Pepper, to taste

BOIL eggs to hard-boiled.
REMOVE shells.
CUT eggs lengthwise.
PUT eggs yolks in bowl; mix with the rest of the ingredients.
CHECK consistency; if not smooth, add a little more mayonnaise.
STUFF eggs.

Salads

Deviled Eggs

6 hard-boiled eggs
2 T. butter
1 T. salad dressing
1/4 tsp. salt
2 1/2 sugar-spoons sugar

1/8 tsp. pepper
3/4 tsp. prepared mustard
Heavy cream, to your
    texture preference

MIX last 6 ingredients together with yolks from eggs. Fill mixture in eggs.
REFRIGERATE.

Dilly Marinated Vegetable Salad

1 c. sugar
1/2 c. vinegar
1/2 c. diced celery
1 can French-cut green
    beans, drained
Miracle Whip

1/2 c. water
1 can mixed vegetables,
    drained
1/2 c. water
1/4 c. diced onion
1/2 tsp. dill weed

DISSOLVE sugar in the water and vinegar.
ADD the 2 cans vegetables.
LET stand in refrigerator overnight.
DRAIN well.
ADD to the remainder of the ingredients.
ADD just enough Miracle Whip to moisten.
TOSS and chill.

Fiesta Salad

Lettuce
Green pepper
Grated Cheddar cheese
Cooked ground beef, sautéed
    with taco seasoning
Sliced black olives

Italian dressing
Tomato
Purple onion
Canned kidney beans
Diced green chilies
Crunched tortilla chips

MIX all ingredients together and serve with portion sizes desired.

Salads

Fire and Ice Tomatoes

3/4 c. vinegar
1/4 c. water
1 1/2 tsp. celery seed
1 1/2 tsp. dill weed
1 1/2 tsp. mustard seed
1/8 tsp. red pepper
1/8 tsp. black pepper
1 T. sugar
1 tsp. garlic

1 cucumber, sliced
1 tsp. salt
6 lg. firm tomatoes, cut into chunks
1 green pepper, cut into strips
1 red onion, cut into rings
3 to 4 celery stalks, sliced

PUT all ingredients, except vegetables, into a saucepan and bring to a boil.
BOIL 1 minute.
PUT vegetables, except cucumber, in a glass bowl.
POUR hot liquid over them, let cool several hours or refrigerate overnight.
WHEN ready to serve, a sliced cucumber can be added.
A good accompaniment to ham or roast.

Freezer Coleslaw

1 med. cabbage, chopped
1 tsp. salt
3 stalks celery
1 c. white vinegar

1/2 c. water
2 c. sugar
1 tsp. mustard seed
1 tsp. celery seed

SPRINKLE salt over cabbage and let stand 1 hour.
MIX cabbage and celery.
MIX remaining ingredients and bring to a boil.
BOIL 1 minute.
COOL.
POUR over cabbage mixture and freeze.

Frozen Fruit Salad

1 (6 oz.) can frozen
   lemonade
1 (6 oz.) can frozen
   orange juice
1 (10 oz.) pkg. frozen
   strawberries

1 can pineapple tidbits
4 to 6 firm, ripe bananas
1/4 to 1/2 c. sugar
1 1/2 c. water

THAW juices and berries (reserving berry juice).
COMBINE all ingredients.
SLICE bananas into mixture last, and mix well.
LINE cupcake pans with cupcake liners.
POUR mixture into cups.
FREEZE.
STORE tightly covered in freezer until ready to serve.

Fruit Salad Dressing

1/2 c. vinegar
1/4 c. honey
1 tsp. paprika
1/2 tsp. celery salt
1 tsp. onion juice

1/4 c. sugar
1 tsp. dry mustard
1/2 tsp. salt
1 tsp. celery seed
1 c. salad oil

MIX first 5 ingredients together and boil for 3 minutes.
COOL and place in a jar.
ADD the remaining ingredients and shake vigorously.
REFRIGERATE.
SHAKE well before using.
SERVE with fresh or frozen fruit.

Salads

Garlic and Herb Dressing

5 cloves garlic, peeled
1/2 c. vinegar
1 tsp. Worcestershire sauce
1 1/2 tsp. rosemary
1 1/2 tsp. black pepper
1 1/2 tsp. celery seed
1 1/2 tsp. sesame seed
2 c. corn oil

1 tsp. paprika
1 tsp. dry mustard
1 tsp. seasoned salt
1 tsp. parsley
1 1/2 tsp. ginger
1 1/2 tsp. basil
1 T. sugar

PUT all ingredients, except oil, in blender. Turn to "chop" for 30 seconds. Then turn to "stir" and gradually drizzle oil into the mixture. BLEND for 2 minutes.
YOU may add or subtract the amount of vinegar to suit your own taste. CHILL 2 hours.
MAY be used on all salads, also when deviling eggs.

Golden Dressing

1/3 c. lemon juice
1/4 c. sugar
1/4 c. orange juice

2 tsp. vinegar
2 eggs

HEAT orange juice to boiling point.
BEAT eggs with sugar until lemon-colored.
ADD hot juice slowly to egg mixture.
COOK in top of double boiler, beating constantly with rotary beater until thick (you may use microwave, heating on high for 1 minute, then stirring. Repeat this step until mixture has thickened).
THIS dressing may be used for fruit, thinning with whipped cream.

BANANA SALAD TO BE USED WITH GOLDEN DRESSING:
6 firm, ripe bananas   1 c. ground peanuts

SLICE bananas and layer in salad dish, one banana at a time; for each layer, drizzle with golden dressing, then ground peanuts, then another layer of sliced bananas.
YOU may make as small or as large a salad as you need.
THIS is a very old, and well-loved recipe.

Salads

Hot Potato Salad

4 c. cooked, sliced potatoes
3 sliced hard-boiled eggs
6 to 8 slices bacon
1/2 c. chopped fresh green
   onions
1 can cream of chicken soup

3 T. vinegar
1/2 tsp. sugar
Dash of pepper
1/4 c. chopped parsley
Dill weed
1/4 c. water

FRY bacon slices until crisp; drain and break up.
ADD to grease, chopped fresh green onions, cream of chicken soup, water, vinegar, sugar and pepper.
MIX and add potatoes, eggs and chopped parsley.
SPRINKLE with dill weed.
SERVE warm.

Macaroni Salad

1 (7 oz.) pkg. macaroni
Salted water
1 c. peas, drained
1/2 lb. cheese, diced
   in squares

1 sm. btl. stuffed olives
6 to 8 sweet pickles, diced
2 pimentos, diced
3 hard-boiled eggs, chopped

MAYONNAISE DRESSING:
1 scant c. sugar
4 T. flour (level)
2 eggs
Generous 1/2 c. vinegar

Pinch of salt
1/2 tsp. prepared mustard
1/2 c. water

BOIL macaroni in salted water.
ADD other ingredients and moisten with homemade salad dressing, which requires 1 pint.

DRESSING:
PUT dressing ingredients in a saucepan and cook. Stir constantly, to prevent sticking, until thickened.
ADD small pieces of butter before it cools.
WHEN cool, add to other ingredients.

Salads

Macaroni-Tuna Salad

3 c. cooked macaroni
1 (6 1/2 oz.) can tuna,
    drained
1 c. diced cheese

1 can peas, drained
1/2 c. chopped celery
3 T. Miracle Whip

MIX ingredients together.
CHILL and serve.

Mushroom-Stuffed Tomatoes

NOTE: If tomatoes are too large or pale, use plum tomatoes instead. You will need 8 to 10; cut in half lengthwise to stuff.

4 lg. or 6 med.-size ripe
    tomatoes
2 T. butter or margarine
1 (8 oz.) pkg. fresh
    mushrooms, chopped
1/4 c. chopped onion
1/2 c. sour cream
2 egg yolks, lightly beaten

1/2 c. fine, dry bread crumbs
1 tsp. salt
1/4 tsp. pepper
1/4 tsp. dried thyme
1 1/2 T. fine, dry bread crumbs
2 or 3 tsp. butter or margarine,
    cut into 4 to 6 pieces

CUT a 1/4-inch slice from tops of tomatoes; scoop out pulp into a bowl, leaving tomato shells intact. Chop enough pulp to measure 1 cup; drain on paper towels. Drain shells upside-down on paper towels. MELT 2 tablespoons butter in a large skillet over medium-high heat; add mushrooms and onion. Cook, stirring constantly, 3 minutes, or until tender.
STIR in 1 cup chopped tomato pulp, sour cream and next 5 ingredients; spoon evenly into tomato shells and place in a greased 8-inch square baking dish. Sprinkle tomato shells evenly with 1 1/2 tablespoons bread crumbs, and dot with 2 to 3 teaspoons butter.
BAKE at 375° for 25 minutes, or until thoroughly heated.
YIELD: 4 servings.

Liberty Red, White and Blue Salad

2 env. unflavored gelatin
1/3 c. sugar
Dash of salt
2 c. milk
1 1/4 c. cottage cheese
1 c. sliced strawberries

1 (8 oz.) can crushed
   pineapple, unsweetened
   juice
1 tsp. grated lemon rind
1/2 c. blueberries

COMBINE gelatin, sugar and salt in a 1 1/2-quart saucepan; stir in 1/2 cup milk.
PLACE over low heat, stirring constantly until gelatin is dissolved; add remaining 1 1/2 cups milk.
STIR in cottage cheese, pineapple and lemon peel.
ARRANGE a few of the strawberries and blueberries in the bottom of an oiled, star-shaped 6-cup mold.
POUR over 1 cup of the gelatin mixture; chill just until set.
ARRANGE some strawberries and blueberries in a design against the side of the mold.
FOLD remaining strawberries and blueberries into gelatin mixture.
TURN into mold and chill until firm.
FROSTED blueberries, green grapes and strawberries make an attractive garnish.
SERVES: 8 to 10.

Salads

Marinated Potato Salad

5 lb. potatoes
1 lg. onion, chopped
1 1/2 c. Miracle Whip
   or mayonnaise

4 eggs, hard-boiled &
   chopped

MARINADE:
2/3 c. salad oil
1/3 c. vinegar
3/4 tsp. salt

1/4 tsp. dry mustard
1/4 tsp. fresh ground or
   salad pepper

MIX marinade and set aside.

BOIL potatoes until tender (approximately 20 to 30 minutes depending upon size). Potatoes should be firm; peel and cut up while hot.

POUR enough marinade over potatoes to dampen. Do not saturate.

ADD chopped onion and mix well.

COVER and let stand at room temperature overnight, stirring occasionally. Add more marinade as required; you will usually have extra marinade, depending on the dryness of the potatoes.

ADD chopped egg and mayonnaise.

REFRIGERATE until ready to serve.

SERVES 12 to 15 generously.

Salads

Pasta-Vegetable Salad

1 (9 oz.) pkg. refrigerated
   cheese-filled tortellini,
   uncooked
3 oz. fettuccine, uncooked
2 c. fresh snow pea pods,
   trimmed
2 c. broccoli flowerets
1 pt. cherry tomatoes, cut
   in half

2 c. sliced fresh mushrooms
1 (7.5 oz.) can pitted whole
   ripe olives, drained
2 T. freshly-grated Parmesan
   cheese
Herbed Pasta Salad
   Dressing (recipe following)
Freshly-grated Parmesan
   cheese, for garnish

COOK tortellini and fettuccine according to package directions; drain and set aside.

COOK snow peas in boiling water to cover 1 minute; remove and plunge peas immediately into cold water to stop the cooking process. Repeat procedure with broccoli.

COMBINE snow peas, broccoli, cherry tomatoes, mushrooms, and olives in a large bowl; add pasta and 2 tablespoons cheese, tossing to combine. Add Herbed Pasta Salad Dressing and toss well. Cover and chill.

GARNISH, if desired.

YIELD: 8 to 10 servings.

HERBED PASTA SALAD DRESSING:

1/2 c. chopped fresh chives
2 T. chopped fresh parsley
2 T. chopped fresh basil
1 T. chopped fresh dill

1/2 tsp. sugar
1/2 tsp. chopped fresh
   oregano
1/2 tsp. Dijon mustard

2 cloves garlic, minced
1 tsp. salt
1/2 tsp. pepper

1/3 c. red wine vinegar
2/3 c. olive oil

COMBINE all ingredients in a jar, cover tightly and shake vigorously.

YIELD: 1 1/4 cups.

Salads

Pickled Carrots

8 c. carrots	1/2 c. salad oil
1/2 c. green pepper, cut fine	1 tsp. salt
1 med. onion, sliced	1 tsp. prepared mustard
1 can tomato soup	1 tsp. Worcestershire sauce
1 c. sugar	1/4 tsp. pepper
3/4 c. vinegar	

COOK carrots until tender; drain and cool. Add green pepper and onion.
COMBINE the rest of ingredients and mix thoroughly; cover.
REFRIGERATE 2 days. Store in refrigerator.

Sweet-Sour Cucumbers

1/2 c. white vinegar	1 tsp. salt
2/3 c. salad oil	1/4 tsp. oregano leaves
2 T. sugar	3 med. cucumbers, thinly sliced

COMBINE all ingredients. Cover and refrigerate for at least 1 hour
before serving.
MAKES 4 cups.

Taffy Apple Salad

4 c. green apples, unpeeled (Granny Smith)	1/2 c. sugar
	1 egg, well beaten
1 (20 oz.) can chunk pineapple	1 1/2 tsp. white vinegar
	1 T. flour
1 1/2 c. cocktail peanuts	1 (8 oz.) ctn. Cool Whip
3 c. mini marshmallows	Top with nuts (opt.)
1/2 c. chopped nuts (opt.)	

DRAIN pineapple and save juice.
MIX pineapple, marshmallows and Cool Whip.
COOK juice, flour, sugar, egg and vinegar until thick.
COOL.
FOLD into first mixture.
ADD apples and peanuts.
TOP with additional nuts, if desired.
CHILL 2 hours.

Salads

FISH AND POULTRY

Fish

BBQ Shrimp Kabobs
Grilled Fish Fillets 53
Grilled Shrimp
Grilled Swordfish with Caper
    Sauce 54
Grilled Trout
Marinated Shrimp 55
Risotto with Shellfish and
    Peas 56
Seafood Gumbo 57
Seafood Pasta 58
Seafood Pasta Salad with
    Curry-Cumin Dressing 59
Seafood Royale Over Green
    Rice 60
Shrimp Spread
Snapper Strips with Banana
    Salsa 61
Sublime Shrimp Salad 62

Poultry

Aloha Chicken 62
Barbecued Raspberry Chicken
Basil Chicken Salad 63
Chicken in Mustard Cream
    Sauce 64
Chicken and Parsley Noodles
    ion White Wine 65
Chicken, Rice and Beans 66
Chicken-Stuffed Green
    Peppers 67

Chicken Packets - Herb
    Chicken 68
Chicken Tortilla Salad
Curried Chicken Salad 69
Dijon Mustard Grilled Chicken
    Breasts 70
Dressed-Up Tropical Chicken
    Salad 71
Easy Marinated Chinese
    Chicken and Pasta
    Salad
Jelly-Glazed Grilled
    Chicken 72
Lemon-Herb Grilled Chicken
Mexican Grilled Chicken 73
Orange Chicken
Picnic-Fried Chicken 74
Pineapple-Glazed Grilled
    Chicken 75
Grilled Chicken Caesar 76
Grilled Turkey Burgers
Grilled Walnut-Rubbed
    Cornish Hens 77
Honey-Gingered Chicken
    Kabobs 78
Honey-Marinade Grilled
    Chicken with Peanut
    Sauce 79
Salsa Chicken
Scalloped Chicken 80
Sesame Ginger Chicken
Zesty Barbecued Chicken 81

List Your Favorite Recipes

Recipes   **Page**

BBQ Shrimp Kabobs

1 lb. lg. shrimp, shelled
  & deveined
1 red bell pepper, seeded &
  cut into 1" chunks
1 yellow bell pepper,
  seeded & cut into
  chunks

1/2 c. smoky barbecue
  sauce
2 T. Worcestershire sauce
2 T. cayenne pepper sauce
1 clove garlic, minced

ALTERNATELY thread shrimp and peppers onto metal skewers; set aside.
STIR together barbecue sauce, Worcestershire sauce, cayenne pepper sauce and garlic. Brush on shrimp.
GRILL for 15 minutes, or until shrimp turn pink, turning and basting often with the sauce.
YIELD: 4 servings.

Grilled Fish Fillets

6 (3/4" thick) fish fillets
1/2 c. butter or margarine
1/4 c. lemon juice
1 T. Worcestershire sauce

1/2 tsp. seasoned salt
1/2 tsp. paprika
1/4 tsp. red pepper

PLACE fillets in a large shallow dish.
COMBINE remaining ingredients in a saucepan; cook, stirring constantly until butter melts.
POUR marinade over fish.
COVER; marinate 1 hour in refrigerator, turning once.
DRAIN fillets, reserving marinade, and place fillets in a fish basket.
GRILL over hot coals 5 minutes on each side or until fish flakes easily when tested with a fork, basting often with marinade.
YIELD: 6 servings.

Fish

Grilled Shrimp

2 lb. unpeeled jumbo fresh
shrimp

3/4 c. butter or margarine,
melted
1/4 c. fresh lime juice

PEEL and devein shrimp.
COMBINE butter and lime juice.
DIP shrimp in butter mixture and thread tail and neck of each shrimp
on skewers so shrimp will lie flat.
GRILL over medium-hot coals 3 to 4 minutes on each side or until
shrimp turn pink.
SERVE butter mixture with shrimp.
YIELD: 4 to 6 servings.

Grilled Swordfish with Caper Sauce

1/2 c. dry white wine
5 cloves garlic, minced
2 tsp. chopped fresh
rosemary, divided
1/4 tsp. salt
1/4 tsp. pepper

4 (4 oz.) swordfish steaks
Vegetable cooking spray
1/3 c. lemon juice
3 T. fine, dry bread crumbs
3 T. extra-virgin olive oil
1 T. capers

COMBINE wine, garlic and 1 teaspoon rosemary in an 8-inch square
baking dish.
SPRINKLE salt and pepper over fish; place fish in baking dish,
turning to coat. Cover and chill at least 1 hour. Remove fish from
marinade, discarding marinade.
COAT food rack with cooking spray; place rack on grill over hot coals
(400° to 500°). Cook, covered with grill lid, 4 to 5 minutes on each side
or until fish flakes easily when tested with fork.
COMBINE remaining 1 teaspoon rosemary, lemon juice and next 3
ingredients. Spoon over fish.
YIELD: 4 servings.

Fish

Grilled Trout

2 T. herb-flavored	2 (2 lb.) dressed trout
vegetable oil	4 sprigs fresh tarragon
1/4 c. lemon juice	1 lemon, sliced
1/2 tsp. salt	Vegetable cooking spray

COMBINE oil, lemon juice and salt in a small bowl, stirring well with a wire whisk. Brush half of mixture inside each trout. Place 2 sprigs tarragon and 2 lemon slices inside each trout.

PLACE trout in a large baking dish. Pour remaining oil mixture over trout. Cover and chill 2 hours.

PLACE trout in a grill basket coated with cooking spray. Cook, covered with grill lid, over hot coals (400° to 500°) for 5 to 7 minutes on each side, or until fish flakes easily when tested with a fork. YIELD: 6 servings.

Marinated Shrimp

6 c. water	1/2 c. tarragon vinegar
2 lb. unpeeled, lg. fresh	2 T. pickling spice
shrimp	1 tsp. salt
Bay leaves	1/2 tsp. dry mustard
4 sm. onions, thinly sliced	Dash of red pepper
& separated into rings	Fresh parsley sprigs
1 c. vegetable oil	

BRING water to a boil; add shrimp and cook 3 to 5 minutes.

DRAIN well; rinse with cold water.

CHILL.

PEEL and devein shrimp, leaving tails intact.

PLACE a layer of shrimp in a flat-bottomed container. Place 5 bay leaves on top of shrimp; cover shrimp with a layer of onion slices. Repeat layering until all shrimp are used.

COMBINE oil and next 5 ingredients, stirring well.

POUR marinade over the shrimp.

COVER; chill 24 hours, stirring mixture occasionally.

REMOVE shrimp from marinade, and arrange in a serving dish.

GARNISH with parsley sprigs.

YIELD: 4 to 6 servings.

Fish

Risotto with Shellfish and Peas

I always use Arborio Rice, as it remains firm in the middle and absorbs more liquid than other types of rice.

3 lb. fresh mussels	2 T. olive oil
2 doz. fresh littleneck clams	1 1/2 c. Arborio rice, uncooked
1 c. dry white wine, divided	1 c. frozen peas, thawed
2 (14 1/2 oz.) cans ready-	1/8 tsp. threads of saffron
to-serve vegetable broth	Pinch of ground red pepper
1 med. onion, finely chopped	1/4 c. chopped fresh parsley
1 clove garlic, finely	1/2 tsp. salt
chopped	1/2 tsp. ground black pepper

SCRUB mussels and clams with a brush, removing any beards from mussels. Discard any opened shells.

BRING 1/2 cup wine to a boil in a large saucepan; add mussels and clams; cook just until shells open. Reserve cooking liquid. Discard any unopened shells. Remove mussels and clams from shells; set aside.

POUR cooking liquid through a fine wire-mesh strainer into a liquid measuring cup, and add enough water to measure 1 cup; return to saucepan. Add vegetable broth; bring to a boil over medium-high heat. Reduce heat and simmer.

COOK onion and garlic in oil in a large saucepan over medium-low heat, stirring constantly, 10 minutes, or until tender (do not brown). ADD rice, and cook over medium-high heat 3 minutes, stirring constantly. Add remaining 1/2 cup wine, and cook until liquid evaporates.

ADD 1/2 cup hot broth mixture to rice; cook, stirring constantly, until liquid is absorbed. Repeat procedure with remaining broth mixture, 1/2 cup at a time. Add peas, saffron and red pepper after 15 minutes.

STIR in mussels, clams, parsley, salt and black pepper.

YIELD: 3 main-dish servings.

Fish

Seafood Gumbo

2 1/2 c. all-purpose flour
1 T. olive oil
2 c. chopped celery
1 c. chopped green bell
    pepper
1 c. chopped green onion
5 cloves garlic, pressed
7 (14 1/2 oz.) cans ready-
    to-serve, no-salt-added,
    fat-free chicken broth
1 T. salt
1/2 tsp. black pepper

1/2 tsp. ground red pepper
1 T. hot sauce
1 (10 oz.) pkg. frozen, cut
    okra
3 lb. unpeeled lg. fresh
    shrimp
2 lb. fresh crabmeat
1 lb. fresh crawfish meat
2 (12 oz.) ctn. fresh
    oysters, undrained
Hot cooked rice
Gumbo filé (opt.)

SPRINKLE flour evenly in 10x15x1-inch pan.
BAKE at 400° for 20 minutes, or until caramel colored (do not burn), stirring often; cool.
POUR oil into a 12-quart stockpot; place over medium heat until hot. Add celery and next 5 ingredients; cook, stirring constantly, 5 to 7 minutes, or until tender.
ADD toasted flour, broth, salt, pepper, red pepper and hot sauce; bring to a boil. Reduce heat and simmer, uncovered, 30 minutes. Add okra and simmer, uncovered, 30 minutes.
PEEL shrimp and devein, if desired. Drain and flake crabmeat, removing any bits of shell.
ADD shrimp, crabmeat, crawfish and oysters to stockpot; cook 15 to 20 minutes, or just until seafood is done. Stir in gumbo filé, if desired.
SPOON over rice and serve immediately.
YIELD: 9 quarts.

Fish

Seafood Pasta

16 lg. shrimp, peeled
   & deveined
1/4 lb. bay scallops
1/4 c. additional seafood
   (crabs, mussels, or
   clams)
3 T. olive oil
1 lg. leek, washed well
   & sliced thinly

6 mushrooms, sliced
2 cloves garlic, minced
6 to 8 sun-dried tomatoes,
   reconstituted & chopped
2 T. white wine
1/2 c. milk
2 T. fresh basil, minced, or
   1/2 tsp. dried
3/4 lb. linguine

WASH shrimp, scallops and additional seafood well, and set aside.
HEAT olive oil in a large skillet. Add leek and mushrooms. Sauté for 4 minutes, stirring frequently. Add garlic and seafood. Cook, stirring frequently, for 3 to 4 minutes.
ADD sun-dried tomatoes and wine. Cook until most of the wine has evaporated.
SPRINKLE flour over mixture; combine well. Cook 1 minute.
ADD milk, stir until thickened. Stir in basil.
MEANWHILE, cook the linguine according to package directions.
DRAIN and place in large bowl.
STIR in seafood sauce.
YIELD: 4 to 6 servings.

Fish

Seafood Pasta Salad with Curry-Cumin Dressing

DRESSING:

3/4 c. mayonnaise
1 1/4 c. yogurt
2 tsp. curry powder

4 tsp. ground cumin
Pinch of ground red pepper, or
more to taste

SALAD:

2 c. cooked seafood (shrimp, scallops or crabmeat)
3 scallions, including a bit of the green part, finely chopped
3 c. cooked pasta, of your choice

8 to 12 cherry tomatoes, cut in half
3 c. mixed greens, torn in half
1/2 c. alfalfa sprouts
1/2 c. toasted almonds

PREPARE the dressing by mixing together mayonnaise, yogurt, cumin, curry powder and red pepper in a medium bowl. Chill.

TO PREPARE SALAD: In a large bowl, combine seafood, scallions, pasta and cherry tomatoes.

ADD enough of the dressing to coat the mixture lightly, and toss well; chill.

WHEN ready to serve, arrange 1/2 cup or so of greens and alfalfa sprouts on 6 plates.

MOUND salad mixture on top of lettuce, and sprinkle with toasted almonds.

YIELD: 6 servings.

Fish

Seafood Royale Over Green Rice

1/2 c. butter	1/3 c. flour
1 1/2 tsp. salt	1/2 tsp. paprika
3 c. milk	1/2 tsp. Worcestershire sauce
4 oz. sliced mushrooms	1/4 c. pimento
1/4 c. chopped parsley	1/2 c. sliced ripe olives
3 c. seafood (albacore tuna, shrimp, crab, or combination)	

COMBINE butter, flour, salt, paprika and milk.
HEAT, stirring, until thickened.
ADD remaining ingredients and heat through.
SERVE on green rice.

GREEN RICE:

2 c. cooked rice	2 egg yolks, beaten
1 c. parsley	1 c. heavy cream
3 green onions	2 egg whites, stiffly beaten
1/3 c. green pepper	

CHOP very fine the parsley, pepper and onion (tops also).
ADD rice, yolks and cream; mix well.
FOLD in beaten egg whites.
POUR into greased 9x9-inch pan, or 1 1/2-quart ring mold.
SET in pan of hot water.
BAKE 45 minutes at 350°, or until set.

Fish

Shrimp Spread

1 (6 oz.) can tiny cocktail
    shrimp, rinsed & drained
1 (8 oz.) pkg. cream cheese,
    softened
1 (10 3/4 oz.) can cream
    of shrimp soup, undiluted

1/4 c. chopped red bell
    pepper
2 T. finely-chopped onion
Dash of hot sauce

CHOP shrimp and set aside.
BEAT cream cheese at medium speed with an electric mixer until
fluffy; gradually add soup, beating well after each addition.
STIR in shrimp, bell pepper and remaining ingredients; chill at least
2 hours. Serve with crackers or toasted French baguette slices.
YIELD: 2 1/2 cups.

Snapper Strips with Banana Salsa

1 1/2 c. crushed potato
    chips
1/4 c. grated Parmesan cheese

1 tsp. ground thyme
1 lb. snapper fillets, cut into strips
1/4 c. milk

COMBINE first 3 ingredients in a shallow dish; dip fish in milk and dredge
in potato chip mixture. Place fish in a single layer on a baking sheet.
BAKE at 500° for 8 to 10 minutes.
YIELD: 8 servings.

BANANA SALSA:
2 med.-size ripe bananas,
    chopped
1/2 c. chopped green bell
    pepper
1/2 c. chopped red bell
    pepper
3 green onions, chopped

1 T. chopped fresh cilantro
2 T. light brown sugar
3 T. fresh lime juice
1 T. vegetable oil
1/4 tsp. salt
1/4 tsp. pepper
1 sm. jalapeño pepper (opt.)

COMBINE first 10 ingredients, stirring gently. Add jalapeño pepper,
if desired. Cover and chill at least 3 hours.
YIELD: 8 servings.

Fish

Sublime Shrimp Salad

8 oz. angel hair pasta
1 c. zucchini, cubed
1/2 med. yellow bell
    pepper, chopped
4 green onions, sliced
12 oz. frozen, cooked
    shrimp, thawed

1/4 c. black olives, chopped
1/2 c. Dijon vinaigrette
    salad dressing
1 c. quartered cherry
    tomatoes
Romaine lettuce

BREAK raw angel hair pasta into thirds. Cook as directed on package; drain. Rinse with cold water.

IN a large bowl, combine pasta, zucchini, bell pepper, onions, shrimp and black olives. Pour dressing over salad and toss gently to coat. Cover and refrigerate 2 hours to allow flavors to blend.

WHEN ready to serve, add tomatoes to salad.

GENTLY toss again and serve on lettuce leaves.

YIELD: 4 (2 cup) servings.

Aloha Chicken

3 c. cubed, cooked chicken
1 green pepper, chopped
1 (22 oz.) can pineapple pie
    filling or thickened,
    crushed pineapple
1/3 c. water

2 tsp. granulated instant
    chicken bouillon
Chow mein noodles
1 1/2 c. sliced celery
3 T. butter
1/8 c. soy sauce

IN saucepan, cook celery and peppers in butter until tender.

ADD remaining ingredients except noodles.

COOK and stir until hot.

SERVE over chow mein noodles.

GARNISH with kiwi fruit, if desired. You may also top each serving with slivered almonds or toasted coconut.

YIELD: 6 servings.

Barbecued Raspberry Chicken

1/2 c. raspberry vinegar
2 T. vegetable oil
1 T. chopped fresh tarragon
4 boneless, skinless chicken
   breast halves (1 lb.)

1 c. undiluted frozen
   raspberry juice
1 T. cornstarch
Pepper, to taste

IN small bowl, combine vinegar, oil and tarragon; mix well and set aside 1/4 cup for basting; cover and refrigerate.
PLACE chicken in a resealable plastic bag or bowl; pour remaining marinade over chicken. Seal or cover and refrigerate for 30 minutes.
LIGHTLY coat cold grill rack with nonstick cooking spray.
DRAIN chicken, discarding marinade.
GRILL, uncovered, 4 inches from hot coals, basting frequently with reserved marinade, for 15 to 18 minutes, or until juices run clear.
MEANWHILE, whisk together juice, cornstarch and pepper in a saucepan.
COOK over medium-low heat, stirring constantly, for 5 to 7 minutes, or until thickened and smooth.
SERVE with chicken.
YIELD: 4 servings.

Basil Chicken Salad

1/2 c. mayonnaise
2 T. lemon juice
1 T. Dijon mustard
1/2 tsp. lemon-pepper
   seasoning
1/4 tsp. hot sauce
3 c. chopped, cooked chicken

1/2 c. chopped celery
1/4 c. shredded fresh basil
2 green onions, chopped
6 c. torn or shredded
   fresh spinach
2 T. pecan pieces, toasted

COMBINE first 5 ingredients, stirring well.
ADD chicken and next 3 ingredients and toss gently.
PLACE spinach on individual serving plates and top with chicken mixture.
SPRINKLE with nuts.
YIELD: 3 servings.

Poultry

Chicken in Mustard Cream Sauce

4 skinned & boned chicken
    breast halves
1/8 tsp. pepper
1 T. Dijon mustard
2 T. olive oil
1/4 c. whipping cream

1/4 c. dry white wine
2 tsp. Dijon mustard
1 tsp. green peppercorns,
    packed in vinegar (opt.)
    (I do not use)

PLACE chicken between 2 sheets of heavy-duty plastic wrap and flatten to 1/4-inch thickness, using a meat mallet or rolling pin. Sprinkle chicken with pepper. Coat 1 side of chicken breast halves evenly with 1 tablespoon mustard.

COOK chicken in oil in a large skillet over medium heat 5 minutes on each side or until chicken is done. Remove chicken from skillet and set aside; keep warm (reserve drippings in skillet).

ADD whipping cream, wine, 2 teaspoons mustard, and, if desired, peppercorns to skillet; cook, stirring constantly, until mixture thickens.

SPOON sauce over chicken.

YIELD: 4 servings.

Poultry

Chicken and Parsley Noodles in White Wine

1 T. olive oil	1 stalk celery, diced
1 lb. boneless, skinless	1 lg. carrot, diced
chicken breast halves,	3 cloves garlic, minced
cut into 1" pieces	Pinch of red pepper flakes
2 tsp. salt	1 (28 oz.) can whole
1/4 tsp. black pepper	tomatoes
1 med. onion, thinly	4 T. thinly-sliced fresh basil
sliced	

WARM oil in large deep skillet over medium-high heat, until hot, but not smoking. Sprinkle chicken pieces with 1 teaspoon of the salt and pepper; cook 3 minutes, until golden brown, stirring often. Remove to plate.

IN the same skillet, still over medium-high heat, cook onion, celery and carrots 5 minutes until softened, stirring. Add garlic, pepper flakes and remaining 1 teaspoon salt; cook 1 minute, stirring. Add tomatoes; bring to a boil. Reduce heat and let simmer 6 minutes, stirring occasionally and breaking up tomatoes with back of spoon.

RETURN chicken to skillet; cook 3 minutes, until chicken is cooked through. Stir in basil.

PARSLEY NOODLES:

COOK 1 package (12 ounces) egg noodles according to package directions; drain.

IN medium serving bowl, toss hot noodles with 2 tablespoons olive oil, 1/4 cup chopped fresh parsley, 1/2 teaspoon salt and 1/4 teaspoon black pepper.

YIELD: 4 servings.

Poultry

Chicken, Rice and Beans

1 T. olive oil
8 chicken drumsticks
   (2 lb.), skin removed
2 c. chicken broth
1 c. chopped onion
1 (7 oz.) bag yellow-rice
   mix
2 tsp. chopped garlic

1 bay leaf
1 (15 1/2 oz.) can pink
   beans, rinsed & drained
1 c. frozen green peas
1 (4 1/2 oz.) can chopped
   green chilies
Chopped parsley & lime wedges,
   for garnish (opt.)

IN nonstick 6-quart Dutch oven, heat oil over high heat; add drumsticks and brown 4 minutes, carefully turning once or twice. Add broth, onion, rice mix, garlic and bay leaf; gently stir to combine. Bring to a boil; reduce heat to medium-low. Cover and simmer 20 minutes.

UNCOVER; gently stir in beans, peas and chilies. Cover and cook 3 minutes, or until peas are hot and chicken is cooked through.

SPOON onto serving plates; garnish with chopped parsley and lime wedges, if desired.

Poultry

Chicken-Stuffed Green Peppers

1 T. margarine or butter
1/2 c. finely-chopped celery
1 (10 3/4 oz.) can condensed
   cream of mushroom soup
1 c. chicken broth
1 single-serving-size
   instant onion soup mix
4 c. cubed, cooked chicken

3 c. hot, cooked rice
5 lg. green sweet peppers
   (about 8 oz.) each
1 tsp. lemon-pepper seasoning
1/4 c. shredded Cheddar
   cheese
1/3 c. pimento

IN a large saucepan, melt margarine or butter over medium heat. Add celery and cook about 5 minutes, or until tender.

STIR in condensed mushroom soup, chicken broth and dry onion soup mix. Heat through. Stir in rice; remove from heat.

TO assemble, halve peppers lengthwise; remove stems, seeds and membranes. Place pepper halves, cut-side up, in a large shallow baking or roasting pan. Divide chicken mixture among the pepper halves. Sprinkle with lemon-pepper seasoning.

COVER peppers loosely with foil.

BAKE in a 350° oven about 25 minutes, or until peppers are crisp and tender. Sprinkle with shredded cheese and top with pimento. Bake, uncovered, about 5 minutes more, or until cheese is just melted.

YIELD: 10 main-dish servings.

THESE stuffed peppers may be made ahead of time.

ASSEMBLE peppers as directed. Cover with foil and refrigerate for up to 24 hours.

TO serve: bake peppers, loosely covered with foil, in a 350° oven about 55 minutes, or until heated through. Top with cheese and pimento. Bake, uncovered, about 5 minutes more, or until cheese is melted.

Poultry

Chicken Packets - Herb Chicken

1/3 c. teriyaki marinade
1 clove garlic, minced
1 tsp. olive oil
1/4 tsp. oregano
1/4 tsp. basil
1 to 1 1/2 lb. boneless,
   skinless chicken breast
   halves, cut in 1/2" strips

1 med. zucchini, thinly sliced
1 med. yellow squash,
   thinly sliced
1 lg. carrot, cut diagonally
   into thin slices
4 sheets heavy-duty
   aluminum foil, 12"x18"
   each

COMBINE all ingredients, toss well to coat chicken.
CENTER 1/4 of mixture on each sheet of heavy-duty aluminum foil.
BRING up sides of foil and double fold. Double-fold ends to form a
packet, leaving room for heat to circulate.
GRILL all packets over medium-hot coals 10 to 12 minutes.
SERVE over white rice.

Poultry

Chicken Tortilla Salad

3/4 c. shredded Monterey
   Jack cheese
1/4 c. mayonnaise, divided
3 T. sour cream
2 T. fresh cilantro
1 T. finely-chopped
   pickled jalapeño peppers
1 clove garlic, minced

4 (4 oz.) skinned & boned
   chicken breast halves
1 (7 oz.) pkg. tortilla chips
9 c. shredded green leaf lettuce
3 Roma tomatoes, thinly sliced
1/4 c. + 2 T. sour cream
Fresh cilantro sprigs, for garnish

COMBINE cheese, 3 tablespoons mayonnaise, 3 tablespoons sour cream and next 3 ingredients; set aside.

PLACE chicken between 2 sheets of heavy-duty plastic wrap and flatten to 1/4-inch thickness, using a meat mallet or rolling pin.

BRUSH both sides of chicken lightly with remaining 1 tablespoon mayonnaise; place on a rack in broiler pan.

BROIL chicken 5 1/2 inches from heat (with electric oven door partially opened), 5 minutes on each side.

SPREAD cheese mixture evenly on top of chicken.

BROIL 3 to 4 additional minutes, or until mixture is browned. Coarsely shred chicken; set aside and keep warm.

LAYER chips, lettuce and tomato evenly on individual plates; top with chicken. Top each serving evenly with sour cream.

GARNISH if desired.

YIELD: 6 servings.

Curried Chicken Salad

2 c. chopped, cooked chicken
1/2 c. chopped celery
1/2 c. sliced, toasted almonds
1/4 c. sliced water chestnuts
1/2 lb. seedless red
   grapes

1 (8 oz.) can pineapple
   chunks, drained
3/4 c. mayonnaise
1 tsp. curry powder
2 tsp. lemon juice
2 tsp. soy sauce

COMBINE first 6 ingredients in a bowl.

COMBINE mayonnaise and next 3 ingredients; spoon over chicken mixture and toss gently.

COVER and chill at least 4 hours.

YIELD: 6 servings.

Poultry

Dijon Mustard Grilled Chicken Breasts

1 T. Dijon mustard
4 chicken breast halves,
    skinned
1/4 tsp. freshly-ground black
    pepper

1/3 c. butter or margarine
2 tsp. lemon juice
1/2 tsp. garlic salt
1 tsp. dried whole tarragon

SPREAD mustard on both sides of chicken and sprinkle with pepper.
Cover and refrigerate 2 to 4 hours.
MELT butter; stir in lemon juice, garlic salt and tarragon.
PLACE chicken on grill over medium coals; baste with butter sauce.
Cover and grill 20 minutes. Remove cover and grill 30 to 35 minutes,
or until done, turning and basting every 10 minutes.
YIELD: 4 servings.

Poultry

Dressed-Up Tropical Chicken Salad

1 1/2 lb. boneless,
   skinless chicken breasts,
   trimmed
1 onion, quartered
2 celery stalks, chopped
   & leaves reserved
1 tsp. Kosher salt
2 med. Granny Smith apples,
   cored & chopped
4 scallions, thinly sliced

3/4 c. red seedless grapes,
   halved
3/4 c. slivered almonds,
   lightly toasted
1 whole fresh pineapple,
   with skin
1 c. mayonnaise
1/4 c. sour cream
1 T. lemon juice
1/8 tsp. salt
1/8 tsp. ground pepper

IN a large saucepan, place chicken breasts and cover with cold water by 1-inch; add onion, celery leaves and Kosher salt.

BRING to a boil; reduce heat to low and simmer for 10 minutes, until chicken is not pink in the center. Remove from liquid and set aside. Discard liquid.

WHEN cool enough to handle, cut chicken into bite-size pieces.

IN a large bowl, mix together chicken, celery, apples, scallions, grapes and almonds.

USE a sharp knife to split pineapple into sixths from top to bottom. Slice core off each pineapple wedge and slice off fruit, leaving tufts of leaves intact. Set aside half the fruit for other use or garnish. Cut the remaining fruit into chunks and add to chicken mixture.

SET pineapple wedges on 6 plates.

IN small bowl, whisk together mayonnaise, sour cream and lemon juice; blend well.

ADD dressing to chicken mixture and toss thoroughly.

ADD salt and spoon mixture onto pineapple wedges.

YIELD: 6 servings.

Poultry

Easy Marinated Chinese Chicken and Pasta Salad

1 c. salad dressing or
   mayonnaise
2 T. reduced-sodium soy
   sauce
1 tsp. ground ginger
1/4 tsp. hot pepper sauce
   (opt.)

3 c. (8 oz.) rotini, cooked &
   drained
2 c. chopped, cooked chicken
1 c. chopped red pepper
1 c. snow pea pods
1/4 c. sliced green onions

MIX salad dressing, soy sauce and seasonings in large bowl.
ADD remaining ingredients; mix lightly.
REFRIGERATE several hours or overnight.
YIELD: 8 servings.

Jelly-Glazed Grilled Chicken

1/4 c. salad oil
1/4 c. cooking sauterne wine
1/4 c. chicken broth
2 T. lemon juice
2 T. apple jelly
1 tsp. salt
1 tsp. flaked parsley

1/2 tsp. prepared mustard
1/2 tsp. Worcestershire sauce
Dash of celery flakes
Dash of pepper
2 ready-to-cook broilers
   (2 1/2 lb.. each), halved
   lengthwise

COMBINE all ingredients except chicken; using rotary beater, beat all the lumps out of jelly.
BRUSH chicken with sauce and place bone-side down on grill.
BROIL over slow coals, turning occasionally and basting frequently, about 1 hour, or until meat is tender and skin is crisp and dark.
YIELD: 4 servings.

Lemon-Herb Grilled Chicken

2/3 c. lemon juice
1/4 c. canned chicken broth
1/4 c. honey
2 T. dried oregano
1 T. dried rosemary
1/2 tsp. salt

1/2 tsp. pepper
3 T. vegetable oil
4 cloves garlic
8 (4 oz.) skinned & boned
    chicken breast halves
Lemon slices, for garnish

COMBINE first 9 ingredients in container of an electric blender and process until smooth, stopping occasionally to scrape down sides.
PLACE chicken in a heavy-duty, zip-top plastic bag; pour lemon juice mixture over chicken. Seal bag, and marinate chicken in refrigerator for 30 minutes.
DRAIN and discard marinade.
COOK chicken, covered with grill lid, over medium-hot coals (350° to 400°) about 5 minutes on each side, or until done, turning occasionally. Garnish, if desired.
YIELD: 8 servings.

Mexican Grilled Chicken

1 (2 1/2 to 3 lb.) frying
    chicken, cut up
1 c. chopped onion
1 c. catsup or chili sauce
    (may use 1/2 c. catsup
    & 1/2 c. salsa)
1/4 c. firmly-packed brown
    sugar

1 clove garlic, crushed
1 T. grated lemon peel
1 tsp. chili powder
1/2 tsp. cumin
2 T. lemon juice
1 T. Worcestershire sauce

HEAT oven to 350°, place chicken on large square of heavy-duty foil; wrap tightly. Roast in foil for 30 minutes.
COMBINE the above ingredients; mix well.
PLACE chicken from foil, skin-side up, on grill; 4 to 6 inches from hot coals.
COOK about 20 minutes, or until done, turning and brushing often with sauce.
YIELD: 4 servings.

Poultry

Orange Chicken

1/4 c. soy sauce
1 tsp. finely-chopped ginger
   root, may use ground
   ginger
1/2 tsp. orange peel
1 T. orange juice

1 lb. boneless, skinless
   chicken breast halves,
   cut into 1/2" strips
2 c. broccoli flowerets
1 med. red bell pepper, cut
   into strips
2 green onions, sliced

COMBINE soy sauce, ginger, orange peel and juice in a small bowl; set aside.

CENTER 1/4 of chicken in single layer on each sheet of aluminum foil. Pour soy sauce mixture evenly over chicken. Arrange vegetables evenly over chicken.

BRING up sides and double foil. Double fold ends, leaving room for heat to circulate.

GRILL each packet for 10 to 12 minutes over medium-high heat, on covered grill.

Picnic-Fried Chicken

1 c. all-purpose flour
2 tsp. pepper
1 tsp. salt
1 tsp. paprika
1/2 tsp. poultry seasoning
1/4 tsp. garlic powder

1 egg, beaten
1/2 c. milk
1 (2 1/2 to 3 lb.) broiler-fryer,
   cut up
Vegetable oil

COMBINE first 6 ingredients in a plastic bag; shake to mix, and set aside. Combine egg and milk; mix well.

SKIN chicken, if desired. Place 2 or 3 pieces in bag; shake well. Dip in egg mixture; return to bag and shake again. Repeat with remaining chicken.

HEAT 1 inch of oil in a large skillet to 350°; add chicken and fry 15 minutes, or until golden brown, turning to brown both sides.

DRAIN on paper towels.

YIELD: 4 servings.

Pineapple-Glazed Grilled Chicken

2 ready-to-cook broiler-
    fryers (about 2 lb.
    each), split in half
    lengthwise

1/2 c. salad oil
2 tsp. salt
1/2 tsp. pepper

PINEAPPLE GLAZE:
1 (9 oz.) can (1 c.) crushed
    pineapple
1 c. brown sugar

2 T. prepared mustard
Dash of salt

BRUSH birds well with oil and season with salt and pepper. Place on grill, with bone side or inside nearest the coals.
BROIL slowly. When bone-side is well-browned, 20 to 30 minutes, turn skin-side down and cook about 20 minutes longer.
BRUSH both sides of birds with Pineapple Glaze and broil about 10 minutes more, or until tender, turning and brushing each side twice with glaze.
PINEAPPLE GLAZE:
DRAIN pineapple, reserving 2 tablespoons syrup.
COMBINE pineapple, reserved syrup, brown sugar, lemon juice, mustard and salt.
YIELD: 1 1/2 cups.
YIELD: 4 servings.

Poultry

Grilled Chicken Caesar

3 T. olive oil	1 lb. boneless, skinless
1 tsp. lemon pepper seasoning	chicken breast
1 tsp. bottled crushed garlic	Flour tortillas
1/4 tsp. oregano	Romaine lettuce, chopped
1/4 tsp. basil	

CAESAR DRESSING:

1 (8 oz.) ctn. sour cream	1/4 tsp. basil
2 T. milk	1/2 tsp. pepper
3 T. Parmesan cheese	1/2 tsp. btl. crushed garlic
1/4 tsp. oregano	

IN a large self-closing plastic bag, combine first 5 ingredients. Add chicken to bag and seal tightly. Turn bag gently to distribute marinade. Refrigerate 15 minutes.

PREHEAT grill to medium heat. Remove the chicken from marinade and arrange on the rack. Grill 10 to 14 minutes, turning occasionally. Remove chicken and cut into strips.

IN a small bowl, combine dressing ingredients. Place romaine and sliced chicken in warmed tortilla. Top with dressing. Fold tortilla. SERVES 4.

SUBSTITUTION: You may substitute chicken with flank or sirloin steak.

Grilled Turkey Burgers

1 lb. ground turkey
1/4 c. seasoned bread crumbs
2 T. chili sauce
1/2 tsp. garlic powder
1/4 tsp. salt
1/2 c. diced onion

1/4 c. sweet pickle relish
1 T. Dijon mustard
1/2 c. chili sauce
1/2 c. Mexican-blend
   shredded cheese

PREHEAT grill to high.
IN medium bowl, lightly toss turkey, bread crumbs, 2 tablespoons chili sauce, garlic powder, pepper, salt, onion, relish and mustard.
FORM mixture into 4 patties.
REDUCE heat on grill to medium-high and place patties on grill grid. Grill 14 to 16 minutes, turning once, or until burgers reach an internal temperature of 160° to 165°.
ABOUT 30 seconds before removing burgers from grill, top each one with 2 tablespoons chili sauce and 2 tablespoons cheese.
SERVE on toasted buns.
YIELD: 4 burgers.

Grilled Walnut-Rubbed Cornish Hens

4 (1 lb.) Rock Cornish
   hens, thawed
1 c. finely-chopped walnuts
   or roasted chestnuts
1/4 c. olive oil
1 tsp. salt

1 tsp. celery salt
1 tsp. poultry seasoning
1/2 tsp. rosemary
1/2 c. butter or margarine,
   melted
Salt & freshly-ground pepper

RINSE birds; pat dry with paper towels. Combine next 6 ingredients; rub half of mixture inside birds.
TRUSS birds; mount on spit, securing with holding forks. Rub birds with remaining nut mixture; let stand 15 minutes.
ROAST over coals 1 to 1 1/4 hours, or until tender. After 15 minutes, brush now and then with butter. Sprinkle with salt and grind pepper over; continue cooking 10 minutes.
YIELD: 4 servings.

Poultry

Honey-Gingered Chicken Kabobs

1 1/2 lb. skinned & boned
    chicken breast halves,
    cut into 1" pieces
1/4 tsp. salt
1/4 tsp. pepper
1 sweet yellow pepper,
    seeded & cut in 1" pieces
1 sweet red pepper, seeded
    & cut into 1" pieces

1 (15 oz.) can or jar baby
    corn, drained & cut in half
1/3 c. hoisin sauce
1/3 c. honey
1/2 tsp. minced fresh ginger,
    or 1/8 tsp. ground ginger
1 clove garlic, crushed

SPRINKLE chicken with salt and pepper. Thread chicken, pepper pieces and corn onto 8 long metal skewers.
COMBINE hoisin sauce and remaining 3 ingredients, stirring well. Brush lightly on kabobs. Grill kabobs, covered with grill lid, over medium-hot coals (350° to 400°) 12 minutes, turning and basting with hoisin sauce mixture.
YIELD: 4 servings.

Honey-Marinade Grilled Chicken
with Peanut Sauce

MARINADE:

1/4 c. soy sauce
2 T. lemon juice or rice
   vinegar
1 T. honey
1 tsp. ground coriander
1/4 tsp. black pepper

1/4 tsp. red pepper flakes
1 clove garlic, minced
1 lb. boneless, skinless
   chicken breasts, cut into
   1" strips

COMBINE all marinade ingredients in a small bowl or in a sealable plastic bag and mix.

ADD chicken and let marinate, refrigerated, several hours or overnight.

PEANUT SAUCE:

3/4 c. chicken broth
1/2 c. peanut butter
1 tsp. sesame oil
1 tsp. soy sauce
1 tsp. lemon juice

1/8 tsp. ground ginger
1/8 tsp. black pepper
1 green onion, finely chopped
1 clove garlic, minced

COMBINE chicken broth and peanut butter in a small bowl; whisk to blend. Stir in remaining ingredients and mix well. Cover and let this mixture stand for at least 1 hour for flavors to blend. (This sauce may be stored in refrigerator for up to 2 days).

TO PREPARE CHICKEN:

WEAVE marinated chicken strips onto skewers.

COOK over hot coals for 3 to 5 minutes per side, or until cooked through, basting frequently with marinade.

SERVE with Peanut Sauce.

Poultry

Salsa Chicken

1 sm. bunch broccoli
1 1/2 c. chopped onion
3 lg. cloves garlic, minced
1 T. olive oil
1 c. chopped red bell pepper
1 lb. skinless, boneless
   chicken breast, cut
   in bite-sized chunks

2 lg. or 3 med. tomatoes,
   diced
1 (16 oz.) can kidney beans
1 c. med.-hot salsa
1/4 c. chopped cilantro (opt.)
Salt & black pepper, to taste

CUT broccoli in bite-sized pieces and steam for 2 to 3 minutes; drain and set aside.

SAUTÉ onion and garlic in oil in large nonstick skillet or Dutch oven for 3 minutes, or until softened. Add bell pepper and sauté 2 minutes.

ADD chicken, tomatoes, broccoli, beans, salsa and cilantro to onion mixture. Over medium heat, bring to a boil; stir lightly, reduce heat and simmer, covered, just until chicken is cooked.

SEASON with salt and black pepper.

SERVE over angel hair pasta.

YIELD: 6 servings.

Scalloped Chicken

8 slices white bread, cubed
1 1/2 c. cracker crumbs,
   divided
3 c. chicken broth
3 eggs
3/4 c. diced celery

2 T. chopped onion
3 c. cubed, cooked chicken
   breast
1 (8 oz.) can sliced mushrooms,
   drained
2 tsp. margarine

IN a bowl, combine bread cubes and 1 cup cracker crumbs.

STIR in broth, eggs, celery, onion, chicken and mushrooms.

SPOON into a 2-quart baking dish, coated with nonstick cooking spray.

IN a saucepan, melt margarine; brown remaining cracker crumbs.

SPRINKLE over casserole.

BAKE at 350° for 1 hour.

YIELD: 8 servings.

Sesame Ginger Chicken

2 T. light soy sauce
2 T. honey
1 T. sesame seeds, toasted
1/2 tsp. ground ginger

4 boneless, skinless chicken
   breast halves (1 lb.)
2 green onions with tops,
   cut into thin strips

COMBINE the first 4 ingredients; set aside.
FLATTEN the chicken breast to 1/4-inch thickness.
GRILL over medium-hot coals, turning and basting frequently with
soy sauce mixture, for 8 minutes, or until juices run clear.
GARNISH with sliced green onions with tops.
YIELD: 4 servings.

Zesty Barbecued Chicken

1/4 c. cooking oil
1/4 c. lime juice
1/4 c. water
2 T. finely-chopped onion
2 tsp. dried tarragon,
   crushed
3/4 tsp. salt
1/2 tsp. ground ginger

1/2 tsp. bottled hot pepper
   sauce
1/4 tsp. garlic powder
1/4 tsp. pepper
4 skinless, boneless med.
   chicken breast halves,
   about 1 lb. total of chicken

MARINADE: In a screw-top jar, add cooking oil, lime juice, water,
onion, tarragon, salt, ginger, pepper sauce, garlic powder and pepper.
COVER and shake well.
RINSE chicken, place in a plastic bag and set in a shallow dish. Pour
marinade over chicken and close bag. Marinate in refrigerator for 1 to
2 hours, turning bag occasionally.
DRAIN the chicken; reserve marinade. Place chicken on rack of an
uncovered grill. Grill directly over medium coals for 12 to 15 minutes,
or until chicken is no longer pink, turning once and brushing with
marinade halfway through. Discard marinade.
YIELD: 4 servings.

Poultry

Notes & Recipes

82   *Poultry*

BEEF AND PORK

Beef

Basil Burgers
Basil-Mozzarella Outdoor
    Burger 83
Beef Kabobs 84
Beef Salad 85
Beef with Sour Cream
Blue Cheese Burgers 86
California Hamburger
Caribbean-Style Steak 87
Double Cheese-Triple Meat
    Burgers
Garden Beef Patties 88
Cheddar Burgers
German Hamburgers 89
Glazed Flank Steak
Grilled Basil-Garlic Steak 90
Grilled Beef Fajitas 91
Grilled Steak with New Orleans-
    Style Butter Sauce
Hamburger with
    Peppercorns 92
Herb Marinated Chuck Steak
Meat Loaf Stuffed
    Peppers 93
New Orleans Hamburger
Oriental Hamburgers 94
Outdoor Burger
Overnight Marinated Flank
    Steak 95
Royal Hamburger 96
Santa Fe Grilled Steak and
    Corn
Spinach Burgers 97
Steak and Spicy Potatoes 98
Steak Salad With Roasted
    New Potatoes 99

Stuffed Beef Tenderloin with
    Mushroom and Wine Sauce
    and Grilled Summer
    Vegetables 100-101
Swiss Cheese Hamburgers ... 101
Tangy Pasta and Beef Salad
Texas Hamburgers 102

Pork

Creole Pork Chops
Zesty Pork Chops 103
Five-Spice Pork 104
Frittata Provolone
Grilled Pork Chops and
    Molasses 105
Grilled Pork Roast with
    Raspberry Salsa
Molasses-Grilled Tenderloin 106
Sausage Burgers 107
Pork Ribs with Pineapple BBQ
    Sauce
Pork Tenderloin in Sour
    Orange Sauce 108
Pork in Tomatillo Chili Sauce
Pork Tenderloin with
    Raspberry Sauce 109
Red Cooked Pork Chops
Rotini with Zucchini and
    Ham 110
Sherried Pork Tenderloins
Sweet and Spicy Pork
    Tenderloin 111
Southwestern Rubbed Ribs .. 112
Sweet Tea-Cured Grilled
    Pork 113
Teriyaki Pork Tenderloin 114

List Your Favorite Recipes

Recipes   **Page**

Basil Burgers

1 1/2 lb. ground sirloin beef	Salt & ground pepper, to
1/4 c. basil pesto	taste
1 lg. clove garlic, minced	6 slices Provolone cheese
1/4 c. oil-packed sun-dried	6 slices tomato
tomatoes, drained &	Thin purple onion slices
minced	6 bagels, onion rolls or
	seed buns, split

COMBINE beef, pesto, garlic, tomatoes, salt and black pepper, mixing thoroughly. Shape into four patties.

BRUSH grill rack with oil. Grill burgers to desired doneness, topping with cheese slices as cooking is completed.

SERVE burgers, topped with tomato slices and onion, on bagels, rolls or buns.

Basil-Mozzarella Outdoor Burger

PREPARE outdoor burger as above, except add 1 slice smoked or regular Mozzarella cheese to each patty during the last 2 minutes of grilling.

SERVE on whole-wheat buns with fresh basil leaves and 1 tablespoon Red Sweet Pepper Relish.

RED SWEET PEPPER RELISH:

1/2 c. purchased roasted red	2 tsp. olive oil
sweet pepper strips	1/4 tsp. pepper
1 T. finely-chopped pitted	1/2 tsp. dried thyme
ripe olives	

IN a food processor bowl, combine red sweet pepper, olive oil, dried thyme and pepper.

COVER bowl and process with several on-off turns, until coarsely chopped.

COVER and chill until ready to serve.

YIELD: 2/3 cup.

Beef

Beef Kabobs

1/2 c. steak sauce	1/2 red bell pepper, diced
1/4 c. red wine vinegar	1 med. onion, quartered
1 T. olive oil	8 sm. to med. mushrooms,
1 (1 1/2 lb.) boneless beef	halved
top round steak, cut into	
1/4" slices	

SOAK 4 (10-inch) wooden skewers in water for at least 30 minutes.
IN small nonmetal bowl, combine steak sauce, vinegar and oil. Use
1/4 cup steak sauce mixture to marinate steak strips for about 1 hour
in the refrigerator. Reserve remaining steak sauce mixture.
COMBINE 1/4 cup reserved steak sauce mixture with red peppers; set
aside.
REMOVE steak slices from marinade; discard marinade. Thread beef
slices on skewers along with 2 mushrooms and 1 onion quarter.
GRILL over medium-high heat for 5 to 8 minutes per side, basting
frequently with remaining 1/4 cup steak sauce mixture.
SERVE warm with red pepper steak sauce mixture.
YIELD: 4 servings.

Beef

Beef Salad

1/4 c. oil
4 tsp. tarragon vinegar
2 tsp. Dijon-style mustard
1/2 tsp. dried tarragon,
   crushed
1/4 tsp. salt
1 lb. boneless beef sirloin
   steak, cut 1" thick
1 c. cauliflower flowerets
1 c. broccoli flowerets

1 sm. red sweet pepper, cut
   into 1" pieces (3/4 c.)
1 sm. yellow sweet pepper,
   cut into 1" pieces (3/4 c.)
1 sm. red onion, halved &
   thinly sliced (1/2 c.)
2 slices bacon, crisp-cooked,
   drained & crumbled
4 c. torn lettuce
1/4 c. finely-shredded
   Parmesan cheese

FOR the dressing: combine oil, vinegar, mustard, tarragon and salt in a screw-top jar. Cover; shake well. Set aside.

SLASH fat on edges of steak at 1-inch intervals. Place steak on the unheated rack of a broiler pan. Boil 3 to 4 inches from the heat to desired doneness, turning once. (Allow 10 to 12 minutes for medium-rare, 12 to 15 minutes for medium.)

YOU MAY GRILL OVER MEDIUM-HOT COALS, IF DESIRED.

CUT the meat into 1-inch cubes.

IN a large mixing bowl, combine the beef, cauliflower, broccoli, peppers, onion and bacon. Toss to mix well.

SHAKE the dressing; pour it over the beef mixture. Toss to coat.

ARRANGE on a dinner plate over lettuce. Sprinkle with Parmesan cheese.

YIELD: 4 servings.

Beef

Beef with Sour Cream

2 T. vegetable oil
1/2 c. beef broth
3 c. cubed beef, browned
    until tender
1/2 c. sour cream

2 med. onions, sliced
1/2 tsp. salt
1/8 tsp. pepper
3 T. Cheddar cheese

SAUTÉ onions in vegetable oil until soft and clear.
ADD beef broth, beef, Cheddar cheese and seasonings.
COVER; simmer gently to heat.
BLEND in sour cream just before serving.
SERVE over cooked noodles.
YIELD: 6 servings.

Blue Cheese Burgers

1/2 lb. fresh mushrooms,
    sliced
2 T. butter or margarine
1 1/2 lb. lean ground beef
1/2 tsp. ground cumin
1/2 tsp. paprika
1/4 tsp. chili powder

1/4 tsp. salt
1/4 tsp. pepper
Pinch of cayenne pepper
2 oz. crumbled blue cheese
2/3 c. barbecue sauce
4 onion rolls or hamburger
    buns, split

IN a skillet, sauté mushrooms in butter for 2 to 3 minutes or until tender. Set aside and keep warm.
COMBINE the beef and seasonings; mix well.
SHAPE into eight thin patties. Sprinkle half with blue cheese. Place remaining patties on top and press edges firmly to seal.
GRILL, uncovered, over medium-hot heat for 3 minutes on each side.
BRUSH with barbecue sauce. Grill 10 to 12 minutes longer or until juices run clear. Serve on rolls with mushrooms on top.
YIELD: 4 burgers.

Beef

California Hamburger

1 lb. ground round or extra-
    lean hamburger
1 (4 oz.) can deviled ham
1/4 tsp. salt
1/4 tsp. black pepper

1/2 c. dry red wine
3 T. butter
2 T. minced parsley
1 T. minced onion

MIX together the beef, ham, salt and onion.
SHAPE into 4 patties.
PLACE in a bowl and add the wine; let marinate in the refrigerator 2 hours. Drain, reserving the wine.
MELT the butter and mix with the wine.
GRILL on medium-hot grill for 14 to 20 minutes, depending on desired doneness. Brush while cooking, with wine-butter mix.
SPRINKLE with parsley and place on buns.

Caribbean-Style Steak

1 1/4 lb. boneless beef chuck
    shoulder or chuck eye
    steaks, cut 1" thick
1/4 c. steak sauce, mixed
    with 1/2 tsp. red pepper
    flakes

2 T. packed brown sugar
2 T. fresh lime juice
Salt, if desired

COMBINE steak sauce mixture, sugar and lime juice; remove and reserve 2 tablespoons marinade for brushing on steak.
PLACE beef steaks in plastic bag; add remaining marinade, turning to coat. Close bag securely and marinate in refrigerator 6 to 8 hours (or overnight, if desired), turning occasionally.
REMOVE steaks from marinade and place on grill over medium coals. Grill 14 to 20 minutes for rare (140°) to medium (160°), turning once.
BRUSH with reserved marinade during last 2 minutes of cooking. Season with salt, if desired.
CUT into thin slices.
YIELD: 4 servings.

Beef

Double Cheese-Triple Meat Burgers

2 lb. ground beef round
4 slices American cheese
Cheddar cheese
4 thick slices cooked ham,
    pan-fried

8 slices bacon, cooked until
    crisp
4 hamburger buns, split
Thousand Island salad
    dressing
4 thick tomato slices

PREPARE charcoal grill. Shape ground round into 4 burgers.
GRILL hamburgers, 6 inches from coals, about 4 minutes on each
side, turning once. Top with a slice of cheese, then ham, and then 2
pieces of bacon crisscrossed. Continue grilling until medium-rare, 2
to 6 more minutes.
SERVE on bun bottom.
SPREAD bun; top with thousand island dressing. Top with tomato
sauce.
SERVE open-faced.

Garden Beef Patties

1 1/2 lb. ground round or
    ground chuck
1 c. cooked potatoes, cut in
    sm. cubes
1 sm. onion, chopped fine
1/4 c. cooked carrots,
    julienned

1/4 c. cooked green bell
    peppers, chopped fine
1 tsp. salt
1 lg. egg
1/4 c. evaporated milk
1/4 tsp. ground black pepper
3 T. butter or margarine
1 celery rib, chopped fine

IN medium bowl, combine ground beef, potatoes, onion, carrots, bell
pepper, egg, evaporated milk, celery, salt and black pepper. Mix
together lightly to form 6 oblong patties.
GRILL 12 to 15 minutes, or until desired doneness, over medium
coals.

Beef

Cheddar Burgers

1 lb. lean ground beef	4 hamburger buns
1 tsp. salt	8 pickle slices (opt.)
1/8 tsp. ground pepper	1 sm. red onion, sliced
1/8 tsp. ground red pepper	1 tomato, sliced
1/2 c. shredded sharp Cheddar	4 lettuce leaves
cheese	4 tsp. ketchup
4 tsp. mayonnaise	

MIX beef, salt and both peppers in a bowl. Shape mixture into 4 (1/2-inch-thick) patties.

GRILL patties over medium-hot coals, 7 minutes on each side or until to desired doneness. Add Cheddar cheese during the last 2 minutes of grilling.

SPREAD 1 teaspoon mayonnaise on bottom of each bun; place burgers on bun; top each with 2 pickle slices (if desired), onion slices, tomato and lettuce. Spread 1 teaspoon ketchup on top of each bun and cover each burger with top of bun.

YIELD: 4 servings.

German Hamburgers

1/2 c. fresh bread crumbs	1/4 tsp. ground pepper
1/2 c. water	1/2 c. thinly-sliced & diced
1 lb. lean ground beef	onion
1 tsp. salt	

SOAK bread in water. Mash smooth, drain and squeeze dry.

MIX together beef, bread, salt, pepper and onion; shape into 4 round patties.

GRILL over medium-hot coals until desired doneness, turning once.

PLACE on hamburger buns and serve.

YIELD: 4 patties.

Beef

Glazed Flank Steak

1 beef flank steak	Orange slices & rosemary
(1 1/2 to 2 lb.)	sprigs

MARINADE:	1 lg. clove garlic, crushed
1 c. prepared teriyaki	1/3 c. honey
marinade	1 T. dark sesame oil
1/3 c. fresh orange juice	Pepper
1 T. chopped fresh rosemary	1/2 c. chopped onion

COMBINE marinade ingredients and pepper to taste; blend well with whisk. Remove and reserve 3/4 cup to use for basting.

LIGHTLY score both sides of steak in a crisscross pattern. Place steak in marinade, turning to coat. Cover and marinate in refrigerator 30 minutes, turning once.

REMOVE steak, discard marinade; place steak over medium-hot coals. Grill, uncovered, 17 to 21 minutes for medium-rare to medium doneness, basting occasionally with reserved marinade. Turn once. Place what remains of the 3/4 cup marinade on grill until boiling. Serve over steak on a platter.

YIELD: 6 servings.

Grilled Basil-Garlic Steak

2 T. olive oil	1 bay leaf
1/2 c. red wine	1/4 tsp. leaf oregano
1 sm. clove garlic, minced	1/4 tsp. dried basil
1 T. minced onion	1 (1 1/2 lb.) boneless sirloin
1/4 tsp. salt	steak, 1" thick
1/2 tsp. black pepper	

COMBINE all ingredients except steak.

TRIM fat from steak. Place steak in dish with tight-fitting lid. Pour marinade over steak and chill, covered, for 8 hours or overnight, turning steak several times.

GRILL steak for about 5 minutes on each side for medium-rare.

THINLY slice steak across grain to serve.

YIELD: 6 servings.

Beef

Grilled Beef Fajitas

1/2 c. steak sauce
1/4 c. lime juice
1 (1 1/2 lb.) boneless beef
   sirloin steak
1 med. onion, thinly sliced
2 red, yellow or green
   peppers, cut into strips

2 (8 1/2" x 11 3/4" x 1/4")
   E-Z foil broiler pans
1 T. olive oil
1/2 tsp. coarsely-ground
   black pepper
6 flour tortillas, warmed

COMBINE steak sauce and lime juice. Use 1/4 cup steak sauce mixture to marinate steak for about 1 hour in the refrigerator. Reserve remaining steak sauce mixture.

PLACE onion and peppers in 1 broiler pan. Toss with 1/4 cup steak sauce mixture, oil and black pepper.

COVER with second foil pan to form a packet. Place on grill over medium heat; cook for 15 to 18 minutes or until vegetables are tender.

MEANWHILE, remove steak from marinade; discard marinade. Grill steak over medium-high heat alongside the vegetable packet for 8 to 10 minutes per side or desired doneness.

THINLY slice steak; add to vegetable mixture. Add remaining steak sauce mixture, tossing to coat well.

SERVE warm with flour tortillas.

YIELD: 6 servings.

Beef

Grilled Steak with
New Orleans-Style Butter Sauce

1 fillet sirloin strip, or
    T-bone steak

STEAK SAUCE:
3 T. salted butter
1 tsp. fresh lemon juice

1 tsp. finely-minced fresh
    parsley
1 1/2 T. Worcestershire sauce

PLACE butter in a small saucepan and turn the heat on to medium under the pan as soon as you put steak over medium-hot coals. Grill 5 to 8 minutes on each side, or to desired doneness.

WHEN almost all the butter has melted, add the remaining ingredients and continue cooking until the sauce turns a light brown, then remove the saucepan from the heat and mix well.

TO SERVE, put the cooked steak on a heated plate. Pour the sauce over and serve.

Hamburger with Peppercorns

2 lb. ground beef round
2 sm. cloves garlic, minced
1 egg, beaten
1 T. brandy
1 T. Dijon mustard
1/3 c. fine, dry bread crumbs

1/2 tsp. freshly-cracked black
    peppercorns
1/4 tsp. ground nutmeg
4 hamburger buns, split
4 thick slices tomato

PREPARE charcoal grill. Mix all ingredients, except buns and tomatoes. Shape into 4 patties.

GRILL until medium-rare or desired doneness, 6 to 10 minutes.

SERVE on buns with sliced tomatoes.

Beef

Herb Marinated Chuck Steak

1 lb. boneless beef chuck
   shoulder steak, cut 1"
   thick
1/4 c. chopped onion
2 T. chopped parsley

2 T. white vinegar
1 T. vegetable oil
2 tsp. Dijon-style mustard
1 clove garlic, minced
1/2 tsp. dried thyme

COMBINE onion, parsley, vinegar, oil, mustard, garlic and thyme.
PLACE beef chuck in plastic bag. Add onion mixture, spreading
evenly over both sides. Close bag securely; marinate in refrigerator 6
to 8 hours (or overnight, if desired), turning at least once.
POUR off marinade; discard.
PLACE steak on grill over medium-hot coals on heavy-duty aluminum
foil for 16 to 18 minutes, turning once.
SERVE with cooked rice or noodles.

Meat Loaf Stuffed Peppers

6 med.-size green bell
   peppers
1 (28 oz.) jar spaghetti
   sauce, divided
2 c. cooked, cubed meat loaf

1 c. cooked rice
1/4 c. diced onion
1/4 c. diced green bell pepper
1/2 c. (2 oz.) shredded sharp
   Cheddar cheese

CUT tops from green peppers and remove seeds.
SPREAD 1 cup spaghetti sauce in bottom of a 7x11-inch baking dish.
Place peppers, cut-side up, over sauce.
STIR together remaining spaghetti sauce, meat loaf and next 3
ingredients in a medium saucepan. Cook over medium heat, stirring
often, 5 to 10 minutes or until thoroughly heated. Spoon evenly into
peppers.
BAKE, uncovered, at 375° for 25 minutes. Sprinkle evenly with
cheese.
YIELD: 6 servings.

Beef

New Orleans Hamburger

1 c. chopped onion
1 T. vegetable oil (opt.)
1 lb. ground beef, preferably
    chuck
1 1/2 tsp. salt

1/2 tsp. ground black pepper
1/8 tsp. cayenne pepper
1/4 tsp. paprika
1/8 tsp. chili powder

FRY the chopped onion in the vegetable oil until glazed and lightly browned.

PLACE the ground beef in a large mixing bowl and add the browned onions and the remaining ingredients. Mix well.

DIVIDE into 4 portions and shape into wide patties about 1/2-inch high.

GRILL over medium-hot coals, flattening with a spatula as they cook. Grill about 5 to 8 minutes on each side, or until at the desired doneness.

SERVE on French bread, garnished with shredded lettuce, sliced tomatoes, pickle slices and mayonnaise.

Oriental Hamburgers

1 lb. lean ground beef or
    ground round
2 T. soy sauce
1/4 tsp. ground pepper

1/2 tsp. ground ginger
1/2 tsp. ground coriander
1/2 c. chopped water
    chestnuts

MIX together all ingredients; shape into 4 patties.
GRILL to desired doneness over medium-hot coals.

Outdoor Burger

1/4 c. finely-chopped onion
2 T. fine, dry bread crumbs
2 T. finely-chopped green
   pepper (opt.)
2 T. catsup
1 T. prepared horseradish
1 T. prepared mustard
1/4 tsp. pepper

1 lb. extra-lean ground beef
4 whole-wheat hamburger
   buns, split & toasted
Shredded radicchio (opt.)
Fresh dill weed (opt.)
Red & yellow cherry tomato
   halves (opt.)

COMBINE onion, bread crumbs, green peppers, catsup, horseradish, mustard, salt and pepper. Add ground beef; mix well. Shape the meat mixture into 4 (3/4-inch) patties.

GRILL patties on an uncovered grill directly over medium coals, for 14 to 18 minutes or until pink remains, turning once halfway through cooking.

SERVE on toasted whole wheat buns with shredded radicchio and fresh dill weed, and red and yellow cherry tomato halves, if desired.

YIELD: 4 servings.

Overnight Marinated Flank Steak

1/4 c. red wine vinegar
1/4 c. canola or extra-virgin
   olive oil
1 onion, minced
2 cloves garlic, minced

1/2 tsp. dried basil
1/2 tsp. dry mustard
1/4 tsp. hot pepper sauce
2 (1 lb.) flank steaks

COMBINE all ingredients except steak and stir until well blended.

PLACE steak in dish. Pour marinade over steak and chill, covered, overnight, turning a few times.

GRILL steak to medium-rare, approximately 4 to 5 minutes per side.

THINLY slice across grain to serve.

YIELD: 8 servings.

Beef

Royal Hamburger

1 sm. white onion	1 1/2 lb. lean ground beef
4 fresh onions	rump
1 T. butter	3 cloves garlic
1/4 c. olive oil	4 hamburger buns
1 tsp. sugar	1/4 lb. Mozzarella cheese
2 sm. seedless tomatoes,	Sprig of parsley, for garnish
or cored beefsteak-	
type tomatoes, peeled &	
crushed	

CUT onions into very thin slices. Fry them in the butter until clear, and set aside.

POUR half of the olive oil into a frying pan and add the sugar and tomatoes. Cook until soft, then reduce heat and set aside tomatoes.

MIX the ground beef with the cooked onions and butter. Form into 4 patties. Set patties aside.

SLICE the garlic cloves into thin strips and fry in the remaining olive oil.

GRILL the patties to desired doneness, covering with Mozzarella cheese on top of pattie last few minutes. Place pattie on the bun and cover with cooked tomatoes and fried garlic slices.

YIELD: 4 servings.

Santa Fe Grilled Steak and Corn

4 beef T-bone or boneless 4 ears fresh sweet corn, in husks
 top loin steaks, cut 1" thick 3 T. butter

GLAZE:
1/2 c. steak sauce   2 tsp. chili powder
2 cloves garlic, crushed   1/2 tsp. ground cumin

PULL back husks from each ear of corn, leaving husks attached to base. Remove corn silk. Fold husks back around corn; tie at end with string or strip of outside corn leaves. Soak in cold water 30 minutes. Drain.
PLACE corn on grill over medium coals; grill, uncovered, 20 to 30 minutes, turning often.
MEANWHILE, combine glaze ingredients; reserve 1/4 cup for chili butter. Place steaks on grill, uncovered; beef T-bone steaks, 15 to 18 minutes (top loin steaks 14 to 16 minutes) for medium-rare to medium doneness, turning once and brushing with glaze.
IN a 1-cup glass measure, add butter to reserved glaze and microwave 1 to 1 1/2 minutes, stirring once. Stir to combine and melt any remaining butter.
REMOVE steaks and corn from grill. Carefully peel away corn husks and brush with chili butter.
SERVE steaks with corn and remaining chili butter.
YIELD: 4 servings.

Spinach Burgers

2 lb. ground round   4 hamburger buns, split,
10 oz. fresh spinach, washed grilled or toasted
4 oz. Monterey Jack cheese, sliced

PREPARE charcoal grill. Shape ground round into 4 burgers.
DROP spinach into boiling water; cook just until bright green. Drain and press out all excess water.
GRILL, turning once, until halfway done, about 4 minutes. Top with some of the drained spinach and a slice of cheese. Press down. Grill until medium-rare, 2 to 6 more minutes.
PLACE on grilled bun. Place bun top next to open-faced hamburger.

Beef

Steak and Spicy Potatoes

1 lb. boneless beef top sirloin
    steak, cut 1" thick
Vegetable cooking spray
2 lg. all-purpose potatoes,
    cut diagonally into 1/2"
    thick slices

1 T. olive oil
3/4 tsp. chili powder
1/8 tsp. ground cumin
1/8 tsp. garlic powder

SPRAY grill rack. Place steak on one side and potatoes on the other side.

COMBINE oil, chili powder, cumin and garlic powder; brush potatoes with half the mixture.

GRILL 16 to 18 minutes until steak is medium-rare to medium and potatoes are tender, turning once; brush potatoes with remaining seasoned oil (you will probably want to use a vegetable basket for the potatoes).

TRIM fat from steak and carve crosswise into slices.

SEASON steak and potatoes with salt and pepper, if desired.

YIELD: 4 servings.

Beef

Steak Salad With Roasted New Potatoes

12 med. cloves garlic,
    peeled
1 lb. new red potatoes, cut
    in half
2 T. olive or salad oil
1 lg. red onion, cut into thin
    wedges
Vegetable cooking spray

3/4 lb. trimmed beef flank
    steak, halved lengthwise,
    cut into thin slices on
    diagonal, across grain
1/4 tsp. black pepper
1/2 tsp. salt
3 T. chicken broth
2 1/2 T. red wine vinegar
6 c. torn salad greens
1/4 c. grated Parmesan cheese

PREHEAT oven to 350°. In large roasting pan, mix together garlic, potatoes and 1 tablespoon of the oil. Roast for 20 minutes longer. Remove to large bowl; reserve roasting pan for dressing (do not clean).

GRILL steak on medium-hot coals in grilling pan, to desired doneness. Sprinkle with 1/4 teaspoon salt and pepper; add to potato mixture in bowl.

IN reserved roasting pan, combine broth, vinegar, remaining 1 tablespoon oil, remaining 1/4 teaspoon salt and any meat juices from grilling pan. Set roasting pan on top of stove over medium-high heat. Bring to a boil, scraping up browned bits; cook for 1 minute.

POUR warm dressing over steak and potato mixture. Add salad greens; toss gently to combine. Divide among plates; sprinkle with Parmesan cheese.

YIELD: 4 servings.

Beef

Stuffed Beef Tenderloin with Mushroom and Wine Sauce and Grilled Summer Vegetables

2 1/2 to 3 lb. beef tenderloin,
    trimmed
1 bunch fresh spinach,
    stemmed & washed
6 oz. fresh button mushrooms
1/4 c. yellow mustard
4 oz. portabello mushrooms

Morton seasoned salt
1/2 lb. lean bacon
1/4 lb. butter
Fresh garlic
1/4 tsp. pepper
1/4 tsp. parsley
1/4 tsp. basil

CUT tenderloin lengthwise 1/2- to 1/4-inch deep, unrolling toward you, slicing and rolling toward you until you've sliced the meat into a rectangle. Layer spinach leaves over the meat.

MELT 1/4 pound butter over low-medium heat. Chop 4 cloves of garlic; dice mushrooms.

COMBINE mustard, garlic, mushrooms, Morton seasoned salt and other spices with melted butter. Let simmer for 15 minutes. Spread mushroom mixture over spinach.

ROLL tenderloin jellyroll fashion and tie. Wrap bacon around it, securing with toothpicks. Place on charcoal grill on top of a pan of water. Cover. Cook until medium-rare (155°).

WINE SAUCE:
1/4 c. butter
2 oz. diced portabello
    mushrooms
2 oz. button mushrooms,
    diced

1/2 c. Burgundy cooking wine
1/4 c. yellow mustard
3 cloves garlic, minced
1/8 tsp. seasoned salt

COOK over coals until wine reduces in half.

WHEN tenderloin reaches 155°, remove from grill. Let stand.

SPOON 2 tablespoons of sauce mixture on a plate.

SLICE tenderloin in between bacon strips so each serving has a piece of bacon wrapped around a slice of meat.

Continued on following page.

Beef

Continued from preceding page.

PLACE a slice of meat on plate, on top of sauce.
SPOON 1 tablespoon sauce over top.
PLACE grilled vegetables next to it.
GARNISH with fresh mushrooms and a sprig of parsley.

GRILLED SUMMER VEGETABLES:

1 red pepper, cut into 1/2" strips

1 green pepper, cut into 1/2" strips

2 zucchini, sliced diagonally, 1/4" thick

1 sweet yellow onion, sliced 1/2" thick

2 yellow squash, diagonally sliced 1/4" thick

2 T. olive oil

1/2 tsp. basil

Juice of 1 lemon

1/2 tsp. seasoned salt

COMBINE all ingredients and refrigerate 1 hour. When tenderloin is done, place a vegetable grill over hot coals. Put on vegetables, turning frequently until done, about 10 minutes.

Swiss Cheese Hamburgers

1 1/2 lb. ground beef

1 1/2 tsp. salt

1/4 tsp. ground pepper

2 T. ice water

6 slices Swiss cheese, cut 1/8" thick

6 slices boiled ham

MIX beef, salt, pepper and water. Shape into 12 patties.
PLACE a slice of cheese and ham on 6 patties, then cover with the remaining patties. Press together gently.
GRILL over medium-hot coals to desired doneness, turning once.
Place on buns and serve.
YIELD: 6 patties.

Beef

Tangy Pasta and Beef Salad

3/4 c. steak sauce
1/3 c. prepared red wine
   vinaigrette salad dressing
3 cloves garlic, chopped
1 (1 lb.) beef top round or
   sirloin steak
3 c. tri-color rotelle pasta,
   cooked & cooled

1/4 lb. piece Swiss cheese,
   cut into matchstick strips
1 c. cherry tomatoes, halved
1 c. broccoli flowerets,
   cooked & cooled
1 c. sliced mushrooms
1/3 c. green onions

IN small nonmetal bowl, combine steak sauce, salad dressing and garlic. Use 1/4 steak sauce mixture to marinate steak for about 1 hour in the refrigerator. Reserve remaining steak sauce mixture for salad dressing.

REMOVE steak from marinade; discard marinade.

GRILL steak over medium heat for 8 to 10 minutes. Thinly slice steak; cut into bite-size pieces.

IN large bowl, combine cooked pasta, steak strips, cheese, tomatoes, broccoli, mushrooms and green onions.

TOSS with half the reserved steak sauce mixture. Chill at least 1 hour to blend flavors.

TO SERVE, stir in remaining steak sauce mixture.

YIELD: 8 to 10 servings.

Texas Hamburgers

1 1/2 lb. ground beef
1/3 c. chili sauce
1/2 c. dry bread crumbs
1 1/4 tsp. salt
1/2 tsp. ground black pepper
2 tsp. chili powder

1/8 tsp. hot sauce
1/4 tsp. dry mustard
2 T. minced onion
1 clove garlic, minced
1/4 c. ice water

MIX all ingredients together; shape into 6 patties.

GRILL 4 minutes on each side, or to desired doneness, turning once.

YIELD: 6 patties.

Creole Pork Chops

4 loin or center-cut pork
    chops, 1 1/2" thick
Salt
Pepper
1 T. salad oil
1/3 c. ketchup
1/2 c. water

1/2 tsp. salt
1/2 tsp. celery seed
3 T. cider vinegar
1/4 tsp. ground ginger
1 tsp. sugar
1 tsp. flour

SPRINKLE chops lightly with salt and pepper.
MIX together remaining ingredients.
MARINATE chops with mixture in plastic bag for 2 to 4 hours.
REMOVE chops. Discard marinade. Grill chops on medium-hot grill 8 minutes on each side, or until meat loses its pink color, or until tender.
YIELD: 4 servings.

Zesty Pork Chops

6 rib pork chops, 3/4" thick
2 T. salad oil
1 tsp. salt
1/2 c. maple-blended syrup
1/2 c. hickory-flavor ketchup
2 T. lemon juice

2 tsp. Worcestershire sauce
1 unpeeled, lg., tart apple,
    cored & cut into 6 rings
1 T. cornstarch
1/3 c. water

BROWN pork chops in salad oil; season with salt. Drain off oil.
COMBINE with syrup, ketchup, lemon juice and Worcestershire sauce. Reserve 1/2 cup mixture; pour remainder over chops. Simmer, covered, over low heat for 25 minutes.
PLACE an apple slice on each chop; top with remaining 1/2 cup sauce mixture. Cover and simmer 25 minutes longer.
REMOVE chops to a hot platter. Blend cornstarch with water and stir into sauce in skillet. Cook, stirring, until sauce comes to a boil and thickens.
SERVE over pork chops.
YIELD: 6 servings.

Pork

Five-Spice Pork

3 T. ground cinnamon
2 tsp. anise seed
1 1/2 tsp. whole black
    peppercorns

1 tsp. fennel seed
1/2 tsp. ground cloves

THESE are the seasonings for your Five-Spice mixture, you may use any remaining blend in your other recipes calling for Five-Spice Seasoning.

1 (12 oz.) pork tenderloin
3 cloves garlic, quartered
    (opt.)

Cooking oil

FOR FIVE-SEASON POWDER: In a blender container, combine the top five seasonings. Blend until powdery.

IF desired, make random cuts about 1/2-inch-deep in meat and insert garlic slices.

BRUSH meat with oil; rub about 1 tablespoon of seasoning blend over the tenderloin. Let stand 30 minutes before grilling.

TO GRILL: arrange medium-hot coals around a drip pan. Place pork over drip pan. Cover and grill for 25 to 30 minutes or until thermometer registers 160° and juices run clear.

REMOVE pork from grill and cover with foil. Let stand 5 minutes before slicing.

YIELD: 4 servings.

Pork

Frittata Provolone

2 T. oil	1/4 tsp. salt
2 tsp. minced garlic	1/8 tsp. pepper
1/2 c. sliced onion	3 T. butter
1/2 c. sliced mushrooms	3/4 c. shredded Provolone
1/2 c. sliced zucchini	cheese
8 eggs	1 c. julienne-sliced cooked
1/2 tsp. basil	ham
1 tsp. oregano	

HEAT oil in a 10-inch skillet. Sauté garlic, onion, mushrooms and zucchini 3 to 5 minutes over medium heat. Remove vegetables from heat.

USING a beater on high speed, beat eggs for 60 to 90 seconds. Combine eggs, sautéed vegetables, ham, basil, oregano, salt and pepper.

MELT butter in skillet. Add egg mixture. Evenly sprinkle shredded Provolone cheese over mixture. Cook over medium heat until eggs are almost set, but center is runny.

REMOVE from heat and place under broiler for 35 to 40 seconds or until top is set and slightly brown. Loosen around edges and slide onto serving dish.

YIELD: 8 servings.

Grilled Pork Chops and Molasses

1/4 c. butter, softened	Salt, to taste
1 T. molasses	4 Iowa chops (1 1/2" thick,
1/2 tsp. fresh lemon juice	boneless, center loin
4 T. coarsely-ground pepper	chops)

MIX together butter, molasses and lemon juice; cover and refrigerate.

RUB chops evenly with pepper.

GRILL chops over medium-hot coals for 12 to 15 minutes, turning once, and topping each chop with butter and molasses mixture.

YIELD: 4 servings.

Pork

Grilled Pork Roast with Raspberry Salsa

2 to 3 lb. single-loin pork
   roast

RASPBERRY SALSA:
1/3 c. chopped onion
1 T. chipotle dried chilies,
   minced

2 T. garlic pepper or lemon
   pepper

1/3 c. raspberry jam (may use
   peach, apricot or cherry
   jam)
1 1/2 T. vinegar
2 T. chopped cilantro

MIX all ingredients well. Place in a small bowl and refrigerate for several hours or overnight.
WARM just before ready to serve over sliced pork roast.

COAT all surfaces of roast with seasoned pepper of your choice. Place roast in heavy-duty aluminum foil in pan over medium coals, with lid on, for 45 minutes to 1 hour. Meat thermometer should read 155°F. After cooking time, remove from grill and let rest 10 minutes.
SERVE with salsa.

Molasses-Grilled Tenderloin

1/4 c. molasses
2 T. coarse-grained Dijon
   mustard

1 T. apple cider vinegar
4 (3/4 lb.) pork tenderloins,
   trimmed

COMBINE the first 3 ingredients; brush over tenderloins. Cover and marinate in refrigerator 8 hours.
COOK, covered with grill lid, over medium-hot coals about 20 minutes or until a meat thermometer inserted in thickest portion registers 160°, turning once.
YIELD: 8 servings.

Sausage Burgers

6 (6") French sandwich rolls
1 1/2 lb. mild Italian link
   sausage
1/4 c. chopped onion
1 lg. egg, lightly beaten
1 tsp. dried oregano

4 red or green bell peppers,
   cut into thin strips
1 med. onion, thinly sliced
2 T. vegetable oil
1/2 tsp. salt
1/8 tsp. pepper
1 T. white vinegar

CUT a 3/4-inch slice from top of each roll; set tops aside.
SCOOP out bottoms of rolls, leaving 1/2-inch shells; tear bread pieces to measure 1/2 cup fresh bread crumbs. Set shells and bread crumbs aside.
REMOVE and discard casings from sausage; crumble sausage into a large bowl. Add reserved bread crumbs, chopped onion, egg and oregano; knead with your hands to mix well. Divide mixture into 6 equal portions and shape into 5x2-inch oval patties.
COOK, covered with grill lid, over medium-hot coals 7 minutes on each side or until done. Remove from grill and keep warm.
COOK bell pepper strips and sliced onion in oil in a skillet over medium-high heat, stirring constantly, 5 minutes or until crisp-tender. Stir in salt, pepper and vinegar; spoon evenly into bread shells. Top with sausage patties and bread tops; serve immediately.
YIELD: 6 servings.

Pork

Pork Ribs with Pineapple BBQ Sauce

3 lb. lean baby back pork ribs
Vegetable cooking spray
1 c. packed brown sugar
2 T. cornstarch
1 (8 oz.) can crushed
    pineapple, undrained
1/2 c. white vinegar
1/4 c. dry sherry or orange juice

2 T. soy sauce
1 T. sesame oil
1 T. finely-chopped fresh
    ginger or 1 1/2 tsp. ground
    ginger
2 lg. cloves garlic, finely
    chopped
2 tsp. salt

PLACE ribs in pan sprayed with vegetable cooking spray; cover.
BAKE at 350° for 45 minutes; drain well.
COMBINE brown sugar and cornstarch until blended, in small sauce-pan. Stir in pineapple, vinegar, sherry, soy sauce, oil, ginger, garlic and salt. Cook over medium heat, stirring until thick and bubbly; set aside.
SPOON pineapple sauce over ribs. Reduce temperature to 325° and bake, uncovered, for 1 hour or more, or until ribs are cooked.

Pork Tenderloin in Sour Orange Sauce

4 pork tenderloins, trimmed
    (4 1/2 to 5 lb.)

MARINADE:

3 c. sour orange juice
    (usually not available,
    the same taste can be
    achieved by combining
    the juice of 2 oranges to
    1 lemon)

1 med. onion, chopped
5 cloves garlic
1/2 c. fresh coriander
1 1/2 c. light Puerto Rican
    rum

MARINATE the tenderloin for 24 hours. Drain, saving 2 cups of the marinade for the sauce. Bake tenderloin at 350° for 15 minutes (until well done). The marinade partially precooks the meat. You may also grill the tenderloin 3 to 5 minutes on each side, or until pinkness is gone.
THICKEN the reserved 2 cups marinade with 2 tablespoons corn-starch mixed with 1/4 cup water. Season with salt and pepper to taste. Serve the pork loin with the sauce.
YIELD: 4 to 6 servings.

Pork in Tomatillo Chili Sauce

2 lb. boneless pork shoulder,
    cut in 1" cubes
1/4 c. all-purpose flour
1/4 c. vegetable oil
1 med.-size onion, chopped
1 (13 oz.) can tomatillos,
    drained & mashed

1 c. chicken broth
1/2 c. chopped cilantro
1/2 c. chopped green chilies
1 tsp. salt
1/4 tsp. black pepper
1 T. dried oregano, crushed
1/2 c. sour cream, for garnish

DREDGE pork in flour, coating all surfaces. Sauté pork in oil until no longer pink.

REMOVE pork from skillet. Drain excess grease and return pork to skillet. Stir in remaining ingredients, except sour cream. Bring to a boil, reduce heat and simmer, covered, for about 45 minutes or until pork is tender.

SERVE over hot steamed rice.

GARNISH individual servings with dollop of sour cream.

YIELD: 8 servings.

Pork Tenderloin with Raspberry Sauce

1 lb. pork tenderloin, trimmed
    & cut into 8 crosswise pieces
Cayenne pepper, to taste

RASPBERRY SAUCE:
6 T. red raspberry preserves
2 T. red wine vinegar
1 T. catsup

2 T. margarine
2 kiwi fruit, peeled & thinly
    sliced

1/2 tsp. horseradish
1/2 tsp. soy sauce
1 clove garlic, minced
Fresh raspberries (opt.)

PRESS each pork tenderloin slice to 1-inch thickness.

LIGHTLY sprinkle both sides of each slice with cayenne pepper. Grill over medium-hot coals 4 to 5 minutes on each side, or until juices run clear.

MEANWHILE, combine all sauce ingredients in small saucepan; simmer over low heat about 3 minutes, stirring occasionally. Keep warm.

PLACE grilled pork slices on warm serving plate. Spoon sauce over; top each pork slice with kiwi slice.

GARNISH serving plate with the remaining kiwi slices and fresh raspberries, if desired.

YIELD: 4 servings.

Pork

Red Cooked Pork Chops

6 (1 1/2" thick) boneless
   pork center loin chops
3 T. brown sugar
3 T. hoisin sauce
3 T. soy sauce
5 tsp. Worcestershire sauce

4 T. sesame oil
2 green onions, minced
1 T. Five-Spice Powder
2 tsp. dried ground ginger
2 cloves garlic, minced

IN small bowl, mix together well all marinade ingredients; place in self-sealing bag along with chops. Seal bag and refrigerate 4 to 24 hours. Drain chops, discarding marinade.
GRILL chops over medium-hot coals in kettle-style grill 7 to 8 minutes; turn and grill 7 minutes more.
YIELD: 6 servings.

FIVE-SEASON POWDER:
3 T. ground cinnamon
2 tsp. anise seed

1 1/2 tsp. whole black
   peppercorns
1 tsp. fennel seed
1/2 tsp. ground cloves

MIX seasonings in blender container; blend until powdery.

Rotini with Zucchini and Ham

6 oz. (1 1/2 c.) uncooked
   rotini
2 T. olive oil
1 c. sliced carrots
1/2 c. chopped onion

2 c. sliced zucchini
1/2 lb. cooked ham, cut into
   2" x 1/2" x 1/4" strips
1/4 tsp. fennel seed

COOK rotini to desired doneness as directed on package; drain. Keep warm.
MEANWHILE, heat oil in large skillet over medium heat until hot. Add carrots and onion; cook and stir 2 to 3 minutes or until crisp-tender. Add zucchini; cook 1 to 2 minutes or until crisp-tender.
STIR in ham and fennel seed; cook 1 to 2 minutes or until thoroughly heated.
ADD rotini to ham mixture; toss gently to combine.
YIELD: 4 (1 1/2-cup) servings.

Sherried Pork Tenderloins

1 lb. pork tenderloin, trimmed
    & cut crosswise into 4
    equal pieces
1/4 c. all-purpose flour
1/4 tsp. salt
1/2 tsp. sugar

1/4 tsp. dried rosemary
    leaves, crushed
1/4 tsp. pepper
2 T. vegetable oil
1 c. dry sherry
1/2 tsp. dry mustard
Roasted red pepper

PRESS each pork tenderloin slice into 1-inch thickness.
IN small bowl, combine flour, salt, sugar, rosemary and pepper; blend well.
COAT both sides of pork slices with flour mixture, shaking off excess flour.
HEAT oil in large skillet over medium heat. Add pork slices; cook 3
to 4 minutes on each side. Remove from skillet, reserving drippings.
Keep warm.
ADD sherry and dry mustard to reserved drippings in skillet. Bring to
a boil over medium heat; stir until mixture is reduced to half. Reduce
heat to low; add cooked pork slices.
SIMMER 1 to 2 minutes; remove from heat.
ARRANGE pork slices on serving plate; spoon half of sauce over slices.
SERVE with roasted red peppers, if desired.
YIELD: 4 servings.

Sweet and Spicy Pork Tenderloin

2 tsp. dried tarragon leaves
1/2 tsp. dried thyme leaves
1/8 to 1/2 tsp. black pepper
Dash of salt

1 lb. pork tenderloin, trimmed &
    cut crosswise into 1/2" pieces
2 T. margarine, melted
1 1/2 T. honey

IN small bowl, combine tarragon, thyme, peppers and salt; blend well.
BRUSH both sides of each pork tenderloin piece with margarine;
sprinkle both sides with seasoning mixture.
GRILL or broil 5 to 6 minutes on each side, using medium-hot heat.
REMOVE from heat.
BRUSH top side of each piece with honey. Grill or broil for an
additional minute.
YIELD: 4 servings.

Pork

Southwestern Rubbed Ribs

4 c. mesquite chips
1 c. catsup
1/2 c. light-colored corn
    syrup
1/4 c. white vinegar
1/4 c. packed brown sugar
1/4 c. finely-chopped onion
2 T. prepared mustard
1 1/2 tsp. Worcestershire
    sauce

2 cloves garlic, minced
1/2 tsp. coarse ground pepper
1/2 tsp. bottled hot pepper
    sauce
1/4 tsp. ground cumin or chili
    powder
1/8 tsp. ground red pepper
Rib Rub
4 lb. pork loin back ribs

AT least 1 hour before grilling, cover chips with water and soak; drain before using. In a 1 1/2-quart saucepan, combine the remaining ingredients, except for Rib Rub and pork loin back ribs. Bring to boiling. Reduce heat and simmer, uncovered, for 25 to 30 minutes, or until thickened, stirring occasionally.

CUT the ribs in serving-size pieces. Pat Rib Rub evenly onto all sides of meat.

IN a covered grill, arrange preheated coals around a drip pan. Put some of the drained wood chips onto the coals. Place ribs on the grill rack over the drip pan.

COVER and grill for 1 1/4 to 1 1/2 hours or until ribs are tender and no pink remains, adding charcoal and chips as needed.

BRUSH with some of the sauce the last 10 minutes of grilling.

YIELD: 6 servings.

RIB RUB: In a blender container or small food processor bowl, combine 2 teaspoons each: dried rosemary (crushed), dried thyme (crushed), dried minced onions, dried minced garlic, 1 teaspoon coarse salt and 3/4 teaspoon pepper. Blend or process until coarsely ground.

Pork

Sweet Tea-Cured Grilled Pork

16 orange pekoe tea bags
2 qt. boiling water
2 c. sugar
1 c. kosher salt
1 c. cider vinegar

2 limes, quartered
8 cloves garlic, crushed
4 (2 1/2 lb.) pork loins,
   trimmed

CURE THE PORK:

STEEP the orange pekoe tea bags in the boiling water until the tea is very strong, about 8 minutes. Remove the tea bags and stir in the sugar, salt and cider vinegar until the sugar and salt are dissolved. Pour into a large container. Add the limes, garlic and 2 quarts of ice water. Add the pork (it should be entirely submerged into the brine). Cover container and refrigerate for 2 days.

COOK THE PORK:

PLACE charcoal on one side of a kettle grill and light. When coals have been burning 20 minutes, place pork on the opposite side of the grill and cook for about 40 to 45 minutes, or until pork registers 135° on an instant-read thermometer.

REMOVE pork from grill and let it rest, covered, for at least 20 minutes. (The temperature will rise.)

SERVE pork sliced into 1/2-inch-thick slices and serve with Sweet Onion Jam.

SWEET ONION JAM:
2 T. butter
4 med. Vidalia or other
   sweet onions, cut into
   3/4" dice

1 c. sugar
2/3 c. dry red wine
2/3 c. red wine vinegar
Salt & pepper, to taste

MELT the butter in a large skillet. Add the onions and cook over moderate heat, stirring until soft and translucent (8 minutes). Add the sugar, wine, vinegar, and a pinch of salt. Cook over low heat, stirring occasionally, until liquid is almost dry (about 40 minutes). Transfer to bowl and season with salt and pepper to taste.

SERVE at room temperature.

Pork

Teriyaki Pork Tenderloin

1 c. teriyaki sauce   2 pork tenderloins, trimmed
2 lg. cloves garlic, pressed

COMBINE teriyaki sauce and garlic in large plastic zipper bag.
ADD tenderloins. Marinate overnight in refrigerator, or for at least 8
hours, turning bag occasionally.
REMOVE tenderloins. Grill over hot coals, or over medium-high heat
on gas grill, for 8 to 10 minutes on each side or to desired doneness.
Tenderloins may be baked at 400° for 30 to 40 minutes.
FOR added zip, add 1 teaspoon finely-grated ginger to marinade.
YIELD: 6 servings.

DESSERTS

Apple-Cream Cheese Tart 115
Cherry Pie 116
Chocolate Cow Patties
Chocolate-Dipped Fruit 117
Coconut Crispies
Creamy Peach Pie 118
Fresh Peach Cobbler
German Chocolate Pie 119
Grilled Apple Melt
Lemon Bars 120
Lemon-Blueberry Cream
    Pie 121

Lemon Meringue Pie 122
Peach-Blueberry Pie
Pound Cake with Strawberries
    and Cream 123
1-2-3-4 Pound Cake 124
Rhubarb Pie 125
Rhubarb Squares
Strawberry Pie 126
Strawberry Tart 127
Three-Layer Bars 128
Wisconsin Apple Pie 129
White Chocolate Fruit Pie 130

List Your Favorite Recipes

Recipes   **Page**

Apple-Cream Cheese Tart

Cream Cheese Pastry
1/2 (8 oz.) pkg. cream
   cheese, softened
1/4 c. sour cream
1 egg yolk
2 T. honey
1/8 tsp. grated lemon rind

1 lg. Granny Smith apple,
   peeled & thinly sliced
1 T. apple jelly
1 1/2 tsp. water
1/2 c. whipping cream
1 1/2 tsp. honey
1/8 tsp. vanilla extract

CREAM CHEESE PASTRY:
1/4 c. butter, cut up
1/2 (8 oz.) pkg. cream cheese,
   cut up

1/4 tsp. salt

COMBINE all ingredients with pastry blender or in a food processor. Shape into a ball; seal in plastic wrap and chill at least 30 minutes (pastry will be dry).
YIELD: Enough for 1 (7 1/2-inch) tart shell.

ROLL Cream Cheese Pastry to 1/8-inch thickness on a lightly-floured surface; fit into a 7 1/2-inch round tart pan with removable bottom. Trim excess pastry along edges; freeze 10 minutes. Line pastry with aluminum foil, and fill with pie weights or dried beans.
BAKE at 400° for 10 minutes. Remove weights and foil and prick bottom of crust with a fork. Bake 10 additional minutes.
COOL on wire rack (pastry will shrink).
BEAT cream cheese and next 4 ingredients in a mixing bowl at medium speed with an electric mixer until smooth. Spoon into tart shell and arrange apple slices on top.
COMBINE apple jelly and water in a small saucepan, cook over low heat, stirring constantly, until jelly melts. Brush half of jelly mixture over apples.
BAKE at 400° on lower oven rack 35 minutes. Cool on wire rack 15 minutes. Brush with remaining jelly mixture; cool.
BEAT whipping cream at medium speed until soft peaks form; stir in 1 1/2 teaspoons honey and vanilla. Serve with tart.
YIELD: 1 (7 1/2-inch tart).

Desserts

Cherry Pie

1 c. sugar
3 T. cornstarch*
1/4 tsp. salt
2/3 c. grenadine syrup
2 (16 oz.) pkg. frozen
    cherries, thawed*

1/2 tsp. almond extract
2 T. butter or margarine
Pastry for double-crust 9" pie
2 tsp. milk

*TWO pounds fresh cherries, pitted, may be substituted for frozen cherries, if desired; use 1/4 cup cornstarch instead of 3 tablespoons cornstarch.

COMBINE first 3 ingredients in a medium saucepan, stirring to remove lumps.

STIR grenadine syrup into sugar mixture. Cook over medium heat until smooth, stirring constantly. Add cherries; simmer until liquid is thickened and transparent (about 4 minutes), stirring gently once or twice. Add almond extract and butter, stirring until butter melts; cool.

ROLL half of pastry to 1/4-inch thickness on a lightly-floured surface. Place in an 9-inch deep-dish pie plate; trim off excess pastry along edges. Pour cooled cherry mixture into pastry shell.

ROLL remaining pastry to 1/8-inch thickness; transfer to top of pie. Trim off excess pastry along edges. Fold edges under and flute. Cut slits in top of crust for steam to escape. Brush top of pastry shell lightly with milk.

BAKE at 400° for 55 minutes, or until golden brown. Cool pie before serving.

YIELD: One 9-inch pie.

Desserts

Chocolate Cow Patties

2 c. margarine, softened
2 c. sugar
2 c. firmly-packed brown
  sugar
4 eggs
2 tsp. vanilla
2 c. quick-cooking oats

2 c. corn flakes
4 c. all-purpose flour
2 tsp. baking powder
2 tsp. baking soda
1 (6 oz.) pkg. semi-sweet
  chocolate morsels
2 c. chopped, broken pecans

CREAM margarine, sugar and brown sugar together until light and fluffy. Add eggs, one at a time, beating well after each addition. Stir in vanilla.
ADD oats and corn flakes to creamed mixture, mixing thoroughly.
SIFT flour, baking powder and baking soda together. Gradually add to creamed mixture, beating slowly to mix. Stir in chocolate morsels and pecans.
DROP by rounded tablespoons onto cookie sheets.
BAKE on top rack of oven at 325° for 17 minutes.
COOL on wire rack.
YIELD: 2 dozen cookies.

Chocolate-Dipped Fruit

1 (12 oz.) pkg. semi-sweet
  chocolate morsels
1/4 c. vegetable shortening

Washed & dried fresh
strawberries or mandarin
orange slices, drained, or
pineapple chunks, drained
or maraschino cherries

OVER hot (not boiling) water, combine chocolate morsels and shortening. Stir until morsels melt and mixture is smooth. Remove from heat, but keep chocolate over hot water. If chocolate begins to set, return to heat and add 1 or 2 teaspoons shortening.
DIP pieces of desired fruit into chocolate mixture, shaking off excess chocolate. Place on foil-lined cookie sheets.
CHILL in refrigerator for 10 to 15 minutes, until chocolate is set. Gently loosen fruit from foil.
YIELD: 18 servings.

Desserts

Coconut Crispies

3/4 c. butter or margarine,
    softened
1 c. sugar
1 egg
1 tsp. vanilla

2 c. all-purpose flour
1/4 tsp. baking powder
1/4 tsp. salt
1 1/2 c. shredded coconut

USING electric mixer, beat butter, sugar, egg and vanilla together until fluffy.

COMBINE flour, baking powder and salt. Add dry ingredients to creamed mixture and beat at low speed just until moistened. Stir in coconut, mixing by hand.

DROP tablespoonfuls of dough onto ungreased cookie sheet, pressing each to 1/4-inch thickness. Using back of fork tines, dipped in flour, to press ridges in each cookie.

BAKE at 375° for 10 to 12 minutes, or until edges are golden.

COOL on wire rack.

YIELD: 3 dozen cookies.

Creamy Peach Pie

1 (3 oz.) pkg. peach-flavored
    gelatin
2/3 c. boiling water
1 c. vanilla ice cream
1 (8 oz.) ctn. frozen
    whipped topping,
    thawed

1 c. diced, peeled fresh
    peaches
1 deep-dish pastry shell
    (9 inches), baked
Sliced peaches &/or mint
    leaves (opt.)

IN a large bowl, dissolve gelatin in boiling water; stir in ice cream until melted and smooth.

ADD whipped topping and mix well. Fold in peaches. Pour into pastry shell.

CHILL until firm, about 3 hours.

IF desired, garnish with peaches and/or mint leaves.

YIELD: 6 to 8 servings.

Desserts

Fresh Peach Cobbler

2 to 3 c. fresh, sliced
    peaches
1 3/4 c. sugar, divided
3 T. butter or margarine,
    softened
1/2 c. milk

1 c. all-purpose flour
1 tsp. baking powder
1/2 tsp. salt, divided
1 T. cornstarch
1 c. boiling water

PLACE peaches in 9x9x2-inch baking pan.
COMBINE 3/4 cup sugar and butter, beating until smooth.
ADD milk, flour, baking powder and 1/4 teaspoon salt to creamed
mixture and mix until smooth. Pour batter over peaches.
COMBINE 1 cup sugar, 1/4 teaspoon salt and cornstarch. Sprinkle
over batter. Pour boiling water over batter.
BAKE at 375° for 1 hour.
YIELD: 9 servings.

German Chocolate Pie

1 (4 oz.) pkg. German
    chocolate
1/4 c. butter or margarine
1 (12 oz.) can evaporated
    milk
1 1/2 c. sugar
3 T. cornstarch

1/8 tsp. salt
2 eggs, lightly beaten
1 tsp. vanilla extract
1 unbaked deep-dish pastry
    shell (9")
1/2 c. chopped pecans
1 1/3 c. flaked coconut

IN a saucepan, melt chocolate and butter over low heat, stirring to mix
well. Remove from the heat and gradually blend in milk; set aside.
IN a bowl, combine sugar, cornstarch and salt. Stir in eggs and vanilla.
Gradually stir in chocolate mixture. Pour into pastry shell.
COMBINE pecans and coconut; sprinkle over filling.
BAKE at 375° for 45 to 50 minutes, or until puffed and browned.
COOL 4 hours.
CHILL (filling will become firm as it cools).
YIELD: 6 to 8 servings.

Desserts

Grilled Apple Melt

2 slices pound cake
Butter, softened
2 slices Cheddar cheese

1/2 c. canned apple pie
filling (you may make
your own)

BUTTER 1 side only of each slice of pound cake.
PLACE 1 slice of cake, buttered-side down, in skillet.
LAYER with 1 slice of cheese, pie filling and remaining slice of cheese.
TOP with second slice of pound cake, buttered-side up.
COOK over low heat, turning carefully, until golden brown on both sides and cheese is melted.
YIELD: 1 serving.
THIS is a great dessert for 1 or for a crowd.

Lemon Bars

CRUST:
1/2 c. butter
1 c. flour

1/4 c. powdered sugar

FILLING:
2 eggs, beaten slightly
2 T. flour
1 c. sugar

2 T. lemon juice & rind
1/2 tsp. baking powder
Top with powdered sugar

MIX crust ingredients very fine. Pat into a 9x13-inch pan.
BAKE 15 minutes at 350°.
MIX filling ingredients well. Pour over crust.
BAKE 25 minutes at 350°.
SPRINKLE with powdered sugar when done.

Desserts

Lemon-Blueberry Cream Pie

1 c. sugar
3 T. cornstarch
1 c. milk
3 beaten egg yolks
1/4 c. butter or margarine
1 T. finely-shredded lemon
   peel

1/4 c. lemon juice
1 (8 oz.) ctn. sour cream
2 c. fresh blueberries
1 (9") baked pastry shell
Sweetened whipped cream
   (opt.)
Lemon slices (opt.)

IN a saucepan, combine 1 cup sugar and cornstarch. Add milk, egg yolks, butter or margarine, and 1 tablespoon lemon peel. Cook and stir over medium heat until thickened and bubbly; cook and stir 2 minutes more.

REMOVE from heat; stir in lemon juice. Transfer to a bowl; cover surface with plastic wrap and refrigerate until cool.

WHEN cool, stir sour cream and blueberries into mixture; pour into pastry shell.

COVER and chill at least 4 hours. If desired, stir a little lemon peel into sweetened whipped cream. Pipe or spoon atop pie.

GARNISH with lemon slices, if desired.

YIELD: 8 servings.

Desserts

Lemon Meringue Pie

1 c. sugar	1/3 c. lemon juice
1/4 c. cornstarch	3 T. butter or margarine
1/4 tsp. salt	1 baked (9") pastry shell
2 c. milk	1/2 tsp. cream of tartar
4 eggs, separated	1/4 c. + 2 T. sugar
1 tsp. grated lemon rind	1/2 tsp. vanilla extract

COMBINE 1 cup sugar, cornstarch and salt in a heavy saucepan. Gradually add milk, stirring until blended. Cook over medium heat, stirring constantly, until mixture thickens and comes to a boil. Boil 1 minute, stirring constantly. Remove from heat.

BEAT egg yolks at high speed of an electric mixer until thick and lemon-colored. Gradually stir about 1/4 of hot mixture into yolks; add to remaining hot mixture, stirring constantly. Cook over medium heat, stirring constantly, 2 to 3 minutes. Remove from heat; stir in lemon rind, lemon juice and butter. Spoon into pastry shell.

BEAT egg whites (at room temperature) and cream of tartar at high speed of an electric mixer 1 minute. Gradually add 1/4 cup plus 2 tablespoons sugar, 1 tablespoon at a time, beating until stiff peaks form and sugar dissolves (2 to 4 minutes). Beat in vanilla. Spread meringue over hot filling, sealing to edge.

BAKE at 350° for 12 to 15 minutes, or until browned.

YIELD: One 9-inch pie.

Desserts

Peach-Blueberry Pie

1 c. sugar
1/3 c. all-purpose flour
1/2 tsp. ground cinnamon
1/8 tsp. allspice
3 c. sliced, peeled fresh
  peaches

1 c. fresh blueberries
Pastry for double-crust
  pie (9")
1 T. butter or margarine
Milk
Cinnamon-sugar

IN a bowl, combine sugar, flour, cinnamon and allspice. Add the peaches and blueberries; toss gently.
LINE pie plate with bottom crust; add the filling. Dot with butter. Top with lattice crust.
BRUSH crust with milk; sprinkle with cinnamon-sugar.
BAKE at 400° for 40 to 45 minutes, or until crust is golden brown and filling is bubbly.
COOL completely.
YIELD: 6 to 8 servings.

Pound Cake with Strawberries and Cream

3 lb. fresh strawberries
3 c. light sour cream

6 T. brown sugar
3 lb. pound cake

RINSE and hull strawberries; slice or leave whole.
WHISK together sour cream and brown sugar until smooth.
CUT cake into about 24 slices.
SERVE each piece with a dollop of the sweetened cream and strawberries on the side. Or, put strawberries and cream in separate bowls alongside the cake platter and let everyone garnish their own.

Desserts

1-2-3-4 Pound Cake

1 c. butter
2 c. sugar
3 c. cake flour (may
    use 2 1/2 c. cake flour
    & 1/2 c. cocoa)

4 eggs
1/2 tsp. salt
3 tsp. baking powder
1 c. sour cream
1 tsp. vanilla

CREAM butter, then add sugar gradually and beat until fluffy. Add eggs, one at a time, beating well after each.

SIFT dry ingredients together.

MIX sour cream and vanilla.

ADD dry ingredients and sour cream mixture alternately to batter, beating well, continuously.

BAKE in a large greased bread pan at 350° for 1 hour.

THIS cake is great by itself, but when used with fresh or canned fruit, is very versatile.

Rhubarb Pie

FOR PASTRY:

1 1/4 c. flour   2/3 c. shortening
1/2 tsp. salt   1/3 c. cold water

FOR FILLING:

3 T. flour   2 c. fresh rhubarb, cut into
1 1/2 c. sugar   sm. pieces*
2 eggs, beaten   1 can cherry pie filling

*YOU may use 4 cups rhubarb, cut in pieces, instead of cherry pie filling.
FOR PASTRY:
COMBINE flour and salt in mixing bowl. Cut shortening into flour
with pastry blender or 2 knives. Do not overmix.
ADD water gradually, sprinkling 1 tablespoon at a time over mixture.
Toss lightly with fork until all particles of flour have been dampened.
Use only enough water to hold the pastry together when it is pressed
between the fingers. It should not feel wet.
DIVIDE the dough into 2 equal portions; roll each into a round ball,
handling as little as possible.
ROLL bottom pastry shell piece out on a lightly-floured board into a circle
1/8-inch thick and 1-inch larger than the diameter of the top of the pan.
FIT circle into a pie plate and trim edges with a scissors or sharp knife.
Let 1/2-inch extend over the rim. Turn edge under and flute with fingers
to make a standing rim. Prick pie shell with a fork to prevent air bubbles.
ROLL out remaining dough for top crust. Decorate top with favorite
design, leaving sufficient holes to allow steam to escape during
baking. Set aside to make pie filling mixture.
TO MAKE FILLING:
COMBINE flour, sugar and eggs; beat thoroughly. Mix in rhubarb
pieces and cherry pie filling, if desired. Pour into pie shell. Moisten
edges of lower crust with cold water and add top crust. Press edges
together tightly with tines of a fork or with fingers.
BRUSH top crust with egg wash (made from 1 egg, beaten with a little
water) and sprinkle with sugar.
BAKE in preheated 425° oven for 15 minutes, then lower oven temperature to 350° and bake for an additional 45 minutes, until golden brown.
YIELD: 1 pie.

Desserts

Rhubarb Squares

2 heaping c. rhubarb	1 egg
1 c. sour cream	2 c. flour
1 1/2 c. brown sugar	1 tsp. baking soda
1 c. butter	1/2 tsp. salt

TOPPING:

1 c. sugar	2/3 c. chopped nuts
1 T. melted butter	1 tsp. cinnamon

CREAM brown sugar, butter and egg.
STIR in flour, baking soda and salt.
MIX in sour cream and rhubarb.
POUR into 9x13-inch pan and spread dough.
THEN top with topping.
BAKE at 350° for 40 to 50 minutes.

Strawberry Pie

3 sq. (1 oz. each) semi-sweet chocolate, divided	1/2 c. sour cream
	3 T. sugar
	1/2 tsp. vanilla extract
1 T. butter or margarine	3 to 4 c. fresh strawberries, hulled
1 (9") pastry shell, baked	
2 (3 oz.) pkg. cream cheese, softened	1/3 c. strawberry jam, melted

IN saucepan, melt 2 ounces chocolate and butter over low heat, stirring constantly; spread or brush over the bottom and up the sides of a pastry shell; chill.
MEANWHILE, in a mixing bowl, beat cream cheese, sour cream, sugar and vanilla until smooth. Spread over chocolate layer; cover and chill for 2 hours.
ARRANGE strawberries, tip-end up, atop the filling. Brush jam over strawberries.
MELT the remaining chocolate and drizzle over all.
YIELD: 6 to 8 servings.

Desserts

Strawberry Tart

2 (3 oz.) pkg. cream
  cheese, softened
1 c. sugar, divided
1/4 c. sour cream

1 1/2 qt. fresh strawberries,
  hulled
Water
1 T. cornstarch
Whipped cream

CRUST:
1 1/2 c. all-purpose flour
1/2 tsp. salt
1/4 c. sugar

1/2 c. vegetable oil
2 T. milk

PREPARE crust by combining flour, salt, sugar, oil and milk, blending well. Press dough into bottom and along sides of 10-inch pie plate. Flute edges and prick bottom and sides of pastry with fork tines.
BAKE at 400° for about 10 minutes; set aside to cool.
BEAT cream cheese until frothy. Add 1 teaspoon sugar and sour cream, beating until smooth. Spread cream cheese mixture in pastry shell and refrigerate.
FORCE 1 rounded cup of strawberries through sieve. Add enough water to measure 1 cup.
COMBINE remaining sugar and cornstarch in a small saucepan. Mix 1/2 cup water with sieved berries and stir into cornstarch mixture. Cook over medium heat, stirring often, until thickened and clear, then boil for 1 minute.
REMOVE from heat, stirring to cool slightly. Add a small amount of red food coloring if necessary.
PLACE remaining berries, tips up, on cream cheese layer in pastry shell. Pour glaze over berries. Chill for 1 hour, or until set.
GARNISH with whipped cream.
YIELD: 8 servings.

Desserts

Three-Layer Bars

STEP 1:

1/2 c. butter

1/4 c. sugar

1/3 c. cocoa

1 tsp. vanilla

1 egg, slightly beaten

2 c. graham cracker crumbs

1 c. grated coconut

1/2 c. chopped nuts

STEP 2:

1/2 c. butter

3 T. milk

2 T. vanilla instant pudding

2 c. powdered sugar

STEP 3:

4 oz. semi-sweet chocolate

1 T. butter

STEP 1:

COOK 1/2 cup butter, cocoa, sugar and vanilla in top of double boiler until blended. Add egg. Cook 5 minutes, stirring constantly. Add graham cracker crumbs, coconut and nuts. Mix and press into 9x9-inch pan. Cool 15 minutes.

STEP 2:

CREAM butter until light. Mix milk and pudding; add to butter. Mix well. Add sugar gradually. Beat and spread over first layer. Let stand in refrigerator 1 hour.

STEP 3:

MELT chocolate and butter; cool. Spread over second layer.
CUT into bars and store in refrigerator.

Desserts

Wisconsin Apple Pie

CRUST:

1 c. all-purpose flour
5 T. butter or margarine
1/2 c. shredded Cheddar
   cheese

1/2 tsp. salt
3 to 4 T. milk

FILLING:

1 (3 oz.) pkg. cream
   cheese, softened
1 egg

1/2 c. sugar
5 c. sliced, peeled baking
   apples

TOPPING:

1/4 c. all-purpose flour
1/4 c. sugar
1/4 tsp. ground cinnamon

2 T. butter or margarine
1/4 c. chopped walnuts or
   hickory nuts

IN a bowl, stir flour, butter, cheese and salt until crumbly. Sprinkle with milk, 1 tablespoon at a time, stirring until pastry holds together; form into a ball. Roll out on a lightly-floured board. Transfer to a 9-inch pie pan; trim and flute edges.

IN a mixing bowl, beat cream cheese, egg and sugar until smooth. Stir in apples; pour into crust.

IN another bowl, mix flour, sugar and cinnamon. Cut in butter until crumbly. Stir in nuts. Sprinkle over apples.

BAKE at 350° for 15 minutes.

REDUCE heat to 300°, bake for 30 to 35 minutes, or until apples are tender.

SERVE warm or chilled, with ice cream if desired.

Desserts

White Chocolate Fruit Pie

6 sq. white chocolate
2 T. milk
4 oz. light cream cheese, softened
1/3 c. powdered sugar
1 tsp. grated fresh orange peel (zest)
1 c. whipping cream, whipped
1 pt. fresh raspberries or strawberries
1 (9") pie crust, baked & cooled

PLACE 5 squares white chocolate and milk in a 2-quart glass measure or bowl. Stirring midway through, microwave on HIGH 2 minutes, or until chocolate melts completely. Cool to room temperature.

USING an electric mixer, in small bowl, beat cream cheese, sugar and zest on low speed until smooth. Beat into melted chocolate. Fold whipped cream into chocolate mixture and spread in cooled pie crust. Place raspberries on filling.

PLACE remaining square of white chocolate in a small freezer-weight plastic bag. Microwave on HIGH 20 seconds; knead chocolate. Repeat until melted. Cut a tiny corner off bag and squeeze melted white chocolate over berries as decoration.

YIELD: 8 servings.

Desserts

FREEZING AND CANNING

Freezing 131-133
Vegetable Freezing
    Chart 134-135
Fruit Freezing Chart 136-137
Apple Butter
Apple Jelly 138
Apricot Pickles
Beet Wine 139
Blackberry Jelly
Blueberry Jam 140
Bread-and-Butter Pickles 141
Calico Vegetable Pickles
Chili Sauce 142
Chow-Chow
Cinnamon Apple Rings 143
Concord Grape Jelly
Corn Relish 144
Cranberry Chutney
Cream-Style Corn 145
Cucumber Refrigerator Pickles
Curry Pickles 146
Dill Pickles
Dilly Beans 147
Easy Sweet Dill Pickles
English Mincemeat 148
Freezer Pickles
Freezer Pickles 149
Freezer Strawberry Jam
Frozen Green Beans 150
Gingered Pears
Green Tomato Pickles 151
Honey-Peach Butter
Horseradish Relish 152
Jalapeño Jelly 153
Kosher Dill Pickles
Lime Pickles 154

Mixed Citrus Marmalade 155
Mom's Two-Week Sweet
    Pickles 156
Okra Pickles
Peach Pickles 157
Peach Preserves
Pepper Jelly 158
Pepper Relish
Perfect Mincemeat 159
Pickled Beets
Quick Grape Jelly 160
Raspberry-Plum Jam
Rhubarb Jam 161
Shortcut Chili Sauce
Spiced Apple Sticks 162
Strawberry Marmalade 163
Strawberry Preserves
Strawberry-Rhubarb Jam 164
Sweet Dill Pickles
Sweet Pickle Relish 165
Tomato Relish
Uncooked Tomato Relish 166
Watermelon Rind Pickles
Zucchini-Pineapple Jam 167
Zucchini Relish 168
Information About Chili
    Peppers 169
Fresh Chili Peppers 170-171
Information on Dried
    Chilies 172-173
Information on Hot Sauces ... 173
Hot Salsa
Salsa 174
Salsa Dressing
Hawaiian Salsa 175
Papaya Corn Salsa 176

List Your Favorite Recipes

Recipes   **Page**

Freezing

EQUIPMENT FOR FRUIT OR VEGETABLES:

Knife	Kitchen scales
Cutting board	Freezer containers (you
Colander	may use bags or rigid
Large measuring container	plastic)

FOR vegetables you will also need:
EQUIPMENT FOR BLANCHING: A blancher or large Dutch oven with a wire mesh basket, and a timer. A large container for cooling the vegetables after blanching.

DIRECTIONS FOR BLANCHING:

HEAT 1 gallon of water to boiling for each pound of prepared vegetables. (Use 2 gallons per pound for leafy green vegetables.) Place vegetables in a blanching basket, and submerge in boiling water. Cover and begin timing when water returns to a boil.

TO stop the cooking process, plunge the basket in ice water, using 1 pound of ice for each pound of vegetables, or hold the vegetables under cold running water. Cool vegetables the same number of minutes recommended for blanching. Drain.

AFTER blanching, freeze vegetables in a dry-pack or a tray pack (for tray pack, spread vegetables in a single layer on a shallow tray, and freeze about 1 hour, or until firm. Then package, leaving no headspace.) (For a dry pack, place cooled vegetables in freezer containers, leaving the recommended headspace, and freeze.)

FOR FREEZING FRUIT:

WASH and drain fruit before peeling, shelling, pitting, or capping; do not soak fruit.

DO NOT use galvanized, copper or iron utensils in preparation of fruit, they may react with the acid from the fruit.

ENZYMES in some fruits cause browning, such as apples, peaches, pears, plums, figs and persimmons. Use a commercial mixture called ascorbic-citric powder, this may be found in any grocery store (there are several brands, they all work well).

Freezing and Canning

HEADSPACE FOR FILLED FREEZER CONTAINERS:
LIQUID pack for vegetables or fruit packed in juice, sugar, syrup or water.)

WIDE-MOUTH CONTAINERS		NARROW-MOUTH CONTAINERS	
PINT	QUART	PINT	QUART
1/2-inch	1-inch	3/4-inch	1 1/2-inches

DRY-PACK for vegetables or fruit, packed without added sugar or liquid.

WIDE-MOUTH CONTAINERS		NARROW-MOUTH CONTAINERS	
PINT	QUART	PINT	QUART
1/2-inch	1/2-inch	1/2-inch	1/2-inch

SUGAR SYRUPS FOR FREEZING FRUIT:

TYPE OF SYRUP	SUGAR (CUPS)	WATER (CUPS)	YIELD (CUPS)
30%	2	4	5
35%	2 1/2	4	5 1/3
40%	3	4	5 1/2
50%	4 3/4	4	6 1/2

DIRECTIONS: Combine the sugar and warm water, stirring until sugar dissolves. Chill.

SYRUP PACK: 40% sugar is recommended for most fruit, a lighter syrup may be used for mild-flavored fruit to keep from masking the flavor. A heavier, sweeter syrup may be needed for tart fruit, such as sour cherries. Use the Sugar Syrups chart for directions for making the different syrup concentrations.
USE just enough cold syrup to cover the fruit, usually 1/2 to 2/3 cup for each pint. Stir dissolved ascorbic acid (your choice of brand) into syrup just before using, to prevent browning, if necessary.
WHEN using rigid containers, place crumpled waxed paper between the fruit and the lid to submerge fruit with syrup. Seal, label, and freeze.

SUGAR PACK: Spread fruit in tray and sprinkle with ascorbic acid dissolved in water, to prevent browning, if necessary.
SPRINKLE fruit with recommended amount of sugar and let stand 10 to 15 minutes to draw out juices and allow the sugar to dissolve. Stir gently to coat fruit, and package with juices. Seal, label, and freeze.

Freezing and Canning

UNSWEETENED PACKS: For a LIQUID PACK, fruit may be frozen unsweetened in water containing ascorbic acid, if needed, or in unsweetened juice. Package as for syrup pack, using chilled liquid. FOR unsweetened DRY PACK, place fruit in containers, leaving recommended headspace and freeze. Ascorbic acid dissolved in water may be sprinkled over fruit before packing if necessary. Fruit pieces can be frozen separately in a TRAY PACK, making it easy to measure fruit without thawing. To prepare a tray pack, spread fruit in a single layer; sprinkle with dissolved ascorbic acid, if necessary. Place tray in freezer, and freeze just until fruit is firm; package, leaving no headspace. Seal, label, and return to freezer.

PACKAGING THE FRUIT: Food will be more convenient to use if packed in amounts to be used for a single meal or recipe. Freezer containers should be no larger than 1/2 gallon capacity; food packed in larger containers freezes too slowly.

Have all food cooled before packing, to help speed freezing. Be sure your syrup or juice for liquid packs is chilled before using. Pack food tightly in containers to leave as little air as possible, but leave enough headspace to allow for expansion during freezing.

WITH freezer bags, press all the air from the bag starting at the bottom, working your way to the top of bag. Use zip-lock or tie bags. IF using rigid plastic containers, keep top edges free of food or moisture to ensure a good seal.

VEGETABLES and most fruits may be kept in the freezer for eight to twelve months.

CITRUS fruit may be kept for four to six months.

Freezing and Canning

Vegetable Freezing Chart

VEGETABLE	PREPARATION	BLANCHING TIME
Beans (butter, lima & pinto)	Choose tender beans with well-filled pods. Shell & wash; sort to size.	Sm. 2 minutes; med. 3 minutes; lg. 4 minutes
Beans (green, snap & wax)	Wash beans, cut off tips lengthwise, 1 to 2".	3 minutes
Corn (on the cob)	Husk, remove silks, trim & wash.	Sm. 7 minutes; med. 9 minutes; lg. 11 minutes
Corn (whole kernel)	Blanch, cut from cob 2/3 depth of kernels.	4 minutes
Corn (cream-style)	Blanch, cut tips, scrape cobs with back of knife to remove juice.	4 minutes
Greens (beet, chard, collards, mustard, spinach, turnip)	Tender, green leaves. Wash thoroughly, remove woody stems.	Collards, 3 minutes; others 2 minutes
Okra	Tender, green pods. Wash, sort to size. Remove stems. Blanch, leave whole or slice.	Small pods, 3 minutes; lg. pods 4 minutes
Peas (black-eyed & field)	Tender pods, shell, wash, discard, hard, small.	2 minutes
Peas (green)	Tender, young peas, shell & wash.	1 1/2 minutes
Peppers (green & sweet red)	Crisp, tender. Wash cut off tops, remove seeds & membrane. Dice, halve or cut in strips 1/2" or rings. Pack raw.	Blanch (optional) Halves 3 minutes. Rings or strips, 2 minutes

Freezing and Canning

Peppers (hot)	Wash, remove stems. Pack leaving no headspace	Not required
Squash (summer)	Young, with small seeds & tender rind. Wash & cut into 1/2" slices	3 minutes
Tomatoes Raw.	Dip in boiling water 30 seconds to loosen skins. Core & peel. Chop or quarter, or leave whole. Pack, leaving no headspace.	Stewed: Remove stem end, quarter. Cover & cook 10 to 20 minutes. Place in cold water-pack.

Freezing and Canning

Fruit Freezing Chart

FRUIT	PREPARATION	TYPE	REMARKS
Apples	Wash, peel & core. For sugar pack, may be blanched 1 1/2 to 2 minutes to retain shape & color.	Syrup 40% Sugar: use 1/2 c. sugar per 1 qt. of apples	To prevent browning, use 1/2 tsp. ascorbic acid per qt. of syrup for syrup pack. Sprinkle 1/4 tsp. ascorbic acid per 1/4 c. water over each qt. sugar pack.
Black-berries, Dewberry Raspberry	Select ripe berries. Wash quickly, remove caps and drain.	Syrup: 40% Sugar: use 3/4 c. sugar per 1 qt. berries. Unsweetened: dry-pack. Purée: 1 c. sugar per 1 qt. puréed berries	Freeze well in unsweetened tray pack.
Blueberry, Huckle-berries	Select fully-ripe berries. For unsweetened pack, do not wash.	Unsweetened: dry-pack. Purée: 1 c. sugar per 1 qt. puréed berries.	Wash, frozen in unsweetened pack before use.
Peaches, Nectarine	Select firm, ripe peaches. Peel; halve or slice.	Syrup: 40% Sugar: Use 2/3 c. sugar per 1 qt. peaches. Unsweetened: liquid pack. Purée: 1 c. sugar 1 qt. puréed peaches.	To prevent browning, use 1/2 tsp. ascorbic acid per qt. syrup for syrup pack or 1 tsp. per qt. water for unsweetened. Sprinkle 1/4 tsp. with 1/4 c. water over each qt. for sugar pack, 1/8 tsp. per qt. purée

Freezing and Canning

Pears	Peel, cut in halves or quarters, remove cores. Heat pears in boiling syrup 1 to 2 minutes. Drain & cool. Chill the syrup.	Syrup: 40%	To prevent browning, use 3/4 tsp. ascorbic acid per qt. of cold syrup.
Plums	Select firm, ripe plums. Sort and wash. Leave whole or cut into halves or quarters; remove pits	Syrup: 40% to 50%	To prevent browning; use 1 tsp. ascorbic acid per qt. of syrup.
Strawberries	Select fully-ripe, firm, deep-red berries. Wash a few at a time; drain & remove caps.	Syrup: 50% Sugar: use 3/4 c. sugar per 1 qt. whole berries.	Strawberries may be crushed or sliced for sugar-pack.
Figs	Select soft-ripe figs. Make sure they are not sour in centers. Sort, wash and cut off stems; do not peel. Halve or leave whole.	Syrup: 35% Unsweetened: dry or liquid pack.	To prevent browning, use 3/4 tsp. ascorbic acid per qt. of syrup for syrup pack or 1 qt. water for unsweetened liquid pack. May use 1/2 c. lemon juice per qt. syrup instead of ascorbic acid.
Persimmons	Select orange-colored, soft, ripe fruit. Peel, cut into quarters, and remove seeds. Press pulp through a sieve to purée.	Sugar: use 1 c. sugar per 1 qt. purée. Unsweetened: dry-pack.	To prevent browning, use 1/8 tsp. ascorbic acid per qt. of purée.

Freezing and Canning

Apple Butter

18 med. tart apples
   (about 6 lb.), quartered
   & cored
3 c. apple juice

3 c. sugar
2 tsp. ground cinnamon
1/2 tsp. ground cloves

IN a large covered kettle, simmer apples in apple juice until tender, about 30 minutes.

PRESS through a sieve or food mill. Return to kettle; boil gently for 30 minutes.

ADD sugar, cinnamon and cloves; cool and stir over low heat for about 1 hour, or until mixture reaches desired thickness, stirring more frequently as it thickens.

POUR hot into hot jars, leaving 1/4-inch headspace. Adjust lids.

PROCESS in boiling-water bath for 10 minutes.

YIELD: 8 half-pints.

Apple Jelly

4 c. apple juice
1 (1 3/4 oz.) pkg. powdered
   pectin

5 c. sugar

COMBINE apple juice and pectin in a large Dutch oven; bring to a boil, stirring occasionally.

ADD sugar, and bring mixture to a full rolling boil. Boil 1 minute, stirring constantly.

REMOVE from heat, and skim off foam with a metal spoon.

QUICKLY pour hot jelly into hot, sterilized jars, leaving 1/2-inch headspace; wipe jar rims. Cover at once with metal lids, and screw on bands.

PROCESS in boiling-water bath for 5 minutes.

YIELD: 7 half-pints.

Freezing and Canning

Apricot Pickles

4 qt. apricots	4 c. brown sugar, firmly packed
Whole cloves	1 qt. vinegar
4 c. sugar	6 (3") sticks cinnamon

STICK each apricot with 2 or 4 cloves.

BRING sugars, vinegar and cinnamon sticks (may be tied in cheese-cloth) to a boil. Add 2 quarts apricots and simmer gently until soft. Remove fruit and repeat with remaining apricots.
REMOVE cinnamon. Fill hot jars with fruit to within 1/2-inch from top; pour on syrup, making certain it covers fruit.
ADJUST lids. Process in boiling-water bath 20 minutes. Remove jars and complete seals.
YIELD: 6 pints.

YOU may substitute peeled peaches or pears for apricots. Use 8 cups white sugar instead of equal parts of white and brown.

Beet Wine

YOU will need a large cooking kettle and 4 1/2 gallons of water. Use enough beets to fill kettle, but still be covered with water.

WHEN you cook your beets, wash clean, then cook as usual.
REMOVE the beets, reserving the water.

4 gal. beet water	2 lb. dark raisins
5 oranges, cut up	3 env. yeast
4 lemons, cut up	8 lb. sugar

PLACE in stone jar in basement, or where cool.
LEAVE nine days.
STIR every day (once).
ON ninth day, strain through a cloth to remove all fruit.
POUR into bottles and leave corks loose.
LET settle for 2 weeks.
RESTRAIN through a fine cloth; rebottle and cork normally.

Freezing and Canning

Blackberry Jelly

About 3 qt. ripe blackberries   2 (3 oz.) pkg. liquid pectin
1 1/2 c. sugar

SORT and wash berries; remove stems and caps. Crush enough berries, and press through a jellybag or cheesecloth to extract 4 cups juice.
COMBINE juice and sugar in a large saucepan, and stir well. Place over high heat; cook, stirring constantly, until mixture comes to a rapid boil. Boil hard 1 minute, stirring constantly. Add pectin, and bring to a full rolling boil; boil 1 minute, stirring constantly. Remove from heat, and skim off foam with a metal spoon.
QUICKLY pour hot jelly into hot sterilized jars, leaving 1/4-inch headspace; wipe jar rims. Cover at once with metal lids, and screw on bands.
PROCESS in a boiling water bath for 5 minutes.
YIELD: 8 half-pints.

Blueberry Jam

1 1/2 qt. stemmed blue-   1 (1") stick cinnamon
   berries, crushed   7 c. sugar
1/4 c. lemon juice   2 (3 oz.) pkg. liquid pectin

COMBINE first 4 ingredients in a Dutch oven; bring to a boil, stirring occasionally, until sugar dissolves. Boil mixture 2 minutes, stirring frequently; remove from heat. Discard cinnamon stick. Add pectin to mixture, and stir 5 minutes. Skim off foam with a metal spoon.
QUICKLY pour hot jam into hot, sterilized jars, leaving 1/4-inch headspace; wipe jar rims. Cover jars at once with metal lids, and screw on bands.
PROCESS in boiling water bath for 10 minutes.
YIELD: 5 half-pints.

Freezing and Canning

Bread-and-Butter Pickles

4 qt. med. cucumbers	5 c. sugar
6 med. onions, sliced	3 c. cider vinegar (5%
2 green peppers, chopped	acidity)
3 cloves garlic	2 T. mustard seeds
1/3 c. pickling salt	1 1/2 tsp. ground turmeric
Crushed ice	1 1/2 tsp. celery seeds

WASH cucumbers, and slice thinly.
COMBINE cucumber, onion, green pepper, garlic and salt in a large Dutch oven. Cover with crushed ice; mix thoroughly, and let stand 3 hours. Drain.
COMBINE remaining ingredients; pour over cucumber mixture. Heat thoroughly, just until boiling. Pack while boiling into hot sterilized jars, leaving 1/2-inch headspace. Remove air bubbles; wipe jar rims. Cover at once with metal lids, and screw on metal bands. Process jars in boiling-water bath for 10 minutes.
YIELD: 8 pints.

Freezing and Canning

Calico Vegetable Pickles

4 c. sliced cucumbers
    (1" slices)
1 1/4 c. sliced carrots
    (1" slices)
2 c. celery (1" slices)
2 c. cubed onions (1" cubes)
2 c. cubed sweet red pepper
    (1" cubes)
1 c. cubed green pepper
    (1" cubes)

1 med. head cauliflower,
    broken into florets (6 c.)
1 c. salt
4 qt. cold water
2 c. sugar
1/4 c. mustard seed
2 T. celery seed
2 T. dried whole black peppers
1 T. dried cilantro
6 1/2 c. vinegar

COMBINE vegetables in a large bowl.
DISSOLVE salt in water and pour over vegetables.
SOAK for 15 to 18 minutes in a cool place. Drain.
IN a large kettle, mix sugar, spices and vinegar. Bring to a boil and boil for 3 to 4 minutes. Add vegetables and simmer 5 to 7 minutes.
PACK hot into 8 hot pint jars, leaving 1/4-inch headspace.
REMOVE air bubbles. Adjust caps; process 15 minutes in boiling-water bath.
YIELD: 8 pints.

Chili Sauce

12 lg. ripe tomatoes,
    chopped
4 lg. onions, chopped
4 lg. green peppers, chopped
    (you may use 2 green
    peppers & 2 red peppers)

1 c. sugar
1 c. vinegar
1 T. cloves
1 T. allspice
2 T. cinnamon
2 T. salt

COMBINE all ingredients and bring to a boil, reduce heat and simmer on low heat for 2 to 3 hours, stirring about every 30 minutes.
PLACE in hot, sterilized jars, leaving 1/2-inch headspace. Wipe rims and screw on bands. Process in boiling water bath for 10 minutes.
YIELD: 12 pints.

Freezing and Canning

Chow-Chow

2 qt. finely-chopped cabbage
1 qt. peeled, chopped green
    tomatoes
6 med. onions, chopped
6 green peppers, coarsely
    chopped
6 red peppers, coarsely
    chopped
1/4 c. pickling salt

6 c. vinegar (5% acidity),
    divided
2 T. prepared mustard
2 1/2 c. sugar
2 T. mustard seeds
1 T. mixed pickling spices
1 1/2 tsp. ground turmeric
1 tsp. ground ginger

COMBINE vegetables and salt; stir well. Cover and let stand 8 hours; drain well.

STIR 2 tablespoons vinegar into mustard. Combine mustard, remaining vinegar and remaining 5 ingredients in a large kettle. Bring to a boil; reduce heat and simmer, uncovered, 20 minutes. Add vegetables; simmer 10 minutes.

SPOON hot mixture into hot, sterilized jars, leaving 1/4-inch headspace. Remove air bubbles; wipe jar rims. Cover at once with metal lids, and screw on bands.

PROCESS in boiling water bath 10 minutes.

YIELD: about 8 pints.

Cinnamon Apple Rings

18 tart apples
6 c. sugar
3 c. water

1 (9 oz.) pkg. red cinnamon
    candies
3 drops red food coloring

CUT cored, peeled apples into rings.

COMBINE sugar, water, cinnamon candies and food coloring. Bring to a boil; boil 3 minutes.

ADD apples to syrup; cook until transparent.

PACK in hot jars. Cover with syrup; adjust lids. Process in boiling water bath 25 minutes. Remove jars from canner and complete seals.

YIELD: 4 pints.

NOTE: Drop rings in lightly-salted water before cooking, to keep them from discoloring. I always use Jonathans.

Freezing and Canning

Concord Grape Jelly

3 1/2 lb. Concord grapes	7 c. sugar
1/2 c. water	1 (3 oz.) pkg. liquid pectin

SORT and wash grapes; remove stems and place in a Dutch oven. Crush grapes and add water. Bring mixture to a boil; cover, reduce heat and simmer 10 minutes. Press mixture through a jelly bag, extracting 4 cups of juice. Cover and let sit 8 hours in a cool place.
STRAIN juice through a double thickness of damp cheesecloth. Combine juice and sugar in a large Dutch oven, and stir well. Place over high heat; cook, stirring constantly, until mixture comes to a rapid boil. Add pectin, and bring to a full rolling boil; boil 1 minute, stirring constantly. Remove from heat and skim off foam with a metal spoon.
QUICKLY pour hot mixture into hot, sterilized jars, leaving 1/4-inch headspace; wipe jar rims. Cover at once with metal lids, and screw on bands.
PROCESS in boiling-water bath 5 minutes.
YIELD: 8 half-pints.

Corn Relish

4 c. fresh, cut corn	1 c. sugar
3 med.-size green peppers, chopped	2 tsp. salt
1 c. chopped onions	1 tsp. whole mustard seeds
1 c. chopped cucumber	3/4 tsp. ground turmeric
1/4 c. chopped celery	1/4 tsp. dry mustard
1 (28 oz.) can whole tomatoes, undrained & chopped	1 1/2 c. vinegar (5% acidity)

COMBINE all ingredients in a large Dutch oven; simmer over low heat 20 minutes. Bring mixture to a boil.
PACK hot mixture into hot, sterilized jars, leaving 1/4-inch headspace. Remove air bubbles; wipe jar rims.
COVER at once with metal lids, and screw on bands.
PROCESS in boiling water bath 15 minutes.
YIELD: 4 pints.

Freezing and Canning

Cranberry Chutney

8 (16 oz.) cans jellied whole-
    berry cranberry sauce
2 c. firmly-packed light
    brown sugar
2 c. chopped dates
2 c. raisins

2 c. slivered almonds
2 c. cider vinegar
1/4 c. minced crystallized
    ginger
2 tsp. ground allspice

COMBINE all ingredients in a large Dutch oven. Bring to a boil, stirring constantly; reduce heat and simmer for 30 minutes, stirring constantly.

COOL, place in jars, and store in refrigerator up to 2 weeks. For longer storage, pack chutney into hot, sterilized jars, filling to 1/2-inch from top; remove air bubbles and wipe jar rims. Cover at once with metal lids, and screw on bands.

PROCESS in boiling-water bath 5 minutes.

YIELD: 10 pints.

THIS is good served over cream cheese with gingersnaps. Also very good with turkey.

Cream-Style Corn

32 freshly-gathered ears of
    corn, or 22 c. fresh corn
1 lb. butter

Salt, to taste
Pepper, to taste
1 pt. half & half

HUSK, wash, cut and scrape corn from the cob, without blanching.

PUT cut corn in a large roaster.

ADD butter, salt, pepper, and half & half.

COVER.

BAKE at 325° for 1 hour, stir often.

COOL quickly by setting pan in ice water.

BAG, label, and freeze.

Freezing and Canning

Cucumber Refrigerator Pickles

8 to 10 cucumbers, cut
    into lg. size pieces
3 lg. onions, sliced
4 c. sugar
1/2 c. salt

1 1/4 tsp. celery seed
4 c. vinegar
1 1/3 c. turmeric
1 1/3 tsp. mustard seed

MIX all together.
KEEP in refrigerator.
STIR every day for 6 days, then pickles are ready to eat.

Curry Pickles

50 cucumbers (med.-sized)
7 T. salt
1 qt. water
1 qt. vinegar

1 T. celery seed
1 T. white mustard seed
1 tsp. curry powder
4 c. sugar

CUT the cucumber in 1/2-inch slices; do not peel.
COVER with water and add the salt. Let stand overnight, then rinse off.
NEXT day, fix the pickling solution of 1 quart water, vinegar, celery seed, mustard seed, curry powder and sugar.
LET the mixture come to a boil; add cucumbers and let boil again.
PACK in hot jars and seal.
YIELD: 7 to 8 quarts.

Freezing and Canning

Dill Pickles

THIS is a very quick way to make dill pickles.

17 to 18 lb. (3" to 5") cucumbers	1/4 c. sugar
1 1/2 c. salt	9 c. water
2 gal. water	2 T. whole pickling spices
6 c. vinegar	Dill heads, fresh or dried
3/4 c. salt	Whole mustard seeds

WASH cucumbers; cover with brine made by adding 1 1/2 cups salt to 2 gallons water. Let stand overnight. Drain.
COMBINE vinegar, 3/4 cup salt, sugar, 9 cups water and pickling spices, tied loosely in cloth bag. Heat to boiling.
PACK cucumbers into hot quart jars. Add 3 dill heads and 2 teaspoons mustard seeds to each jar. Pour boiling vinegar mixture, spice bag removed, over cucumbers to within 1/2-inch of jar tops. Place lid on jars, screw metal band on jars. Process in boiling-water bath 20 minutes.
REMOVE jars from canner, retighten jar lids and allow to seal.
YIELD: 7 quarts.

Dilly Beans

2 dried whole red peppers	2 c. cider vinegar
2 cloves garlic	2 c. water
2 sm. heads dill	1/4 c. canning salt
1/4 tsp. alum	

PUT in bottom of quart jar: red peppers, garlic, dill and alum.
PACK jars with whole green beans.
HEAT cider vinegar, water and canning salt.
FILL jars with brine and seal.

Freezing and Canning

Easy Sweet Dill Pickles

2 qt. dill pickles, sliced
   (8 to 10 pickles)
4 cloves garlic, crushed
   (opt.)
2 1/3 c. vinegar

2 T. allspice
1 T. peppercorns
4 c. sugar
1 c. brown sugar, firmly
   packed

DRAIN dill pickles.
MAKE a pickling syrup of garlic, vinegar, spices and sugars. Simmer 5 minutes. Add pickle slices; heat to a boil.
PACK in hot jars; adjust lids. Process in boiling-water bath 5 minutes.
REMOVE jars and complete seals.
YIELD: 2 quarts.

English Mincemeat

1/2 lb. lean ground beef
6 apples, peeled & chopped
1 1/2 c. brown sugar
1 c. dark seedless raisins
1 c. apple juice or cider

3 tsp. grated orange peel
3 tsp. cinnamon
2 tsp. salt
1 tsp. cloves
1/2 c. brandy or rum

COOK all ingredients, except brandy, stirring occasionally.
ADD brandy. Cook over low heat for 30 minutes.
PROCESS in boiling-water bath for 1 hour. Remove jars and allow to seal.
YIELD: 5 cups.

Freezing and Canning

Freezer Pickles

1 c. green peppers, chopped
1 c. onions, sliced

8 c. cucumbers, sliced
1 T. pickling salt

BRINE:
1 T. celery salt
1/2 tsp. turmeric

2 c. vinegar
2 c. sugar

COMBINE peppers, onions and cucumbers with salt and let stand at least 3 hours, mixing occasionally.
COMBINE brine ingredients and bring to a boil. Cool.
DRAIN liquid from cucumbers.
MIX brine with drained cucumbers.
PACK in plastic containers.
COVER tightly and freeze.
YIELD: 5 to 6 pints.

Freezer Pickles

PICKLES:
7 c. cucumbers, thinly
    sliced
1 c. onions, sliced or chopped

Cold water, to cover
    cucumbers
2 T. pickling salt

SUGAR MIXTURE:
2 c. sugar
1 c. vinegar

1 tsp. celery seed

MIX pickling salt with cucumbers and onion.
COVER with cold water and leave overnight.
NEXT morning, drain and discard liquid.
MIX sugar, vinegar and celery seed. Stir very well, and pour over pickles.
PLACE in freezer containers and freeze.
ONCE frozen they may be used at anytime.
YIELD: 5 to 6 pints.

Freezing and Canning

Freezer Strawberry Jam

3 c. crushed strawberries
5 c. sugar
3/4 c. water

1 (1 3/4 oz.) pkg. powdered
pectin

COMBINE strawberries and sugar; let stand 20 minutes, stirring occasionally.

COMBINE water and pectin in a small saucepan; bring to a boil. Boil 1 minute, stirring constantly. Add to fruit, and stir 3 minutes.

QUICKLY spoon into freezer containers or hot, sterilized jars, leaving 1/2-inch headspace. Cover at once with plastic or metal lids, and screw on bands.

LET stand at room temperature 24 hours; freeze.

YIELD: 7 half-pints.

Frozen Green Beans

1 gal. water
1/2 c. vinegar

1/2 c. canning salt
1 gal. fresh green beans

BRING to a boil water, vinegar and canning salt.

ADD 1 gallon beans. Bring to a boil again.

BOIL for 10 minutes.

SPOON beans into jar, 1/2-inch from top.

ADD juice and seal.

Freezing and Canning

Gingered Pears

4 lb. fresh pears
1/3 c. finely-chopped ginger
   root (2 oz.)
1/4 c. fresh lemon juice

5 c. sugar
2 tsp. grated lemon peel
1/4 c. vinegar

WASH, peel, quarter and core pears. (If extra large, cut them into eighths.)
SOAK ginger in lemon juice while soaking pears.
ADD sugar to pears and mix well to coat each piece. Cover and let stand overnight, or 6 to 8 hours.
STIR lemon-soaked ginger into pears.
COOK, uncovered, over medium-low heat until pears are tender and clear, about 1 hour, stirring frequently. (Cooking time depends upon ripeness of pears.) Add lemon peel and vinegar 5 minutes before cooking time is up.
PACK in hot jars, filling to within 1/2-inch from top. Adjust lids. Process in boiling water bath 20 minutes. Remove jars and complete seals.
YIELD: 7 half-pints.
THIS is great with meat, but especially good on toast.

Green Tomato Pickles

Select sm. firm green
   tomatoes & leave
   stems on

WASH and pack in sterilized quart jars.
TO each quart, add the following:

1 clove garlic
1 stalk celery

1 hot green or red pepper
1 head dill

COMBINE:

1 qt. vinegar
2 qt. water

1 c. salt

COOK 5 minutes.
POUR hot over contents in jars, to 1/2-inch of top.
SEAL.

Freezing and Canning

Honey-Peach Butter

10 lb. peaches, peeled	1 1/2 c. sugar
& chopped	1 1/2 c. honey
1/2 c. water	

IN a large kettle, cook the peaches in water until soft.
PRESS through a sieve or food mill.
MEASURE 12 cups pulp; return to kettle. Add sugar and honey.
COOK, stirring often, until mixture thickens, about 1 1/4 hours. Stir more frequently as it thickens, to prevent sticking.
POUR hot into jars, leaving 1/4-inch headspace.
ADJUST caps.
PROCESS for 10 minutes in a boiling-water bath.
YIELD: 6 pints.

Horseradish Relish

1 3/4 lb. fresh horseradish	1 1/2 c. boiling vinegar
1/2 tsp. salt, divided	(5% acidity)

SCRUB horseradish root; peel and cut into 2-inch pieces.
POSITION knife blade in food processor bowl; add horseradish. Top with cover and process until finely chopped.
PACK horseradish into hot, sterilized jars. Add 1/4 teaspoon salt to each jar.
POUR boiling vinegar into jars, covering horseradish, leaving 1/4-inch headspace. Remove air bubbles; wipe jar rims. Cover at once with metal lids and screw on bands.
PROCESS in boiling water bath 10 minutes.
YIELD: 2 pints.
MIXTURE will separate after storage; stir well before using.

Freezing and Canning

Jalapeño Jelly

THIS is a small recipe to keep in refrigerator. You may increase the recipe, process in a boiling-water bath for 10 minutes for long-term storage.

3 fresh jalapeño peppers,
    seeded & coarsely
    chopped
1/2 green bell pepper,
    coarsely chopped

3 c. sugar
1/2 c. cider vinegar
1/2 (6 oz.) pkg. liquid fruit
    pectin
2 T. fresh lime juice

POSITION knife blade in food processor bowl; add jalapeño and bell peppers. Process until smooth, stopping once to scrape down sides.
COMBINE pepper purée, sugar and cider vinegar in a large nonaluminum saucepan. Bring mixture to a boil over medium-high heat, stirring constantly. Boil 3 minutes; stir in pectin and lime juice. Boil 1 minute, stirring constantly. Remove from heat, and skim off foam with a metal spoon.
POUR into hot, sterilized jars, filling to 1/4-inch from top; wipe jar rims. Cover at once with metal lids, and screw on bands; cool.
STORE in refrigerator.
SERVE over cream cheese with crackers. May also use with meats as a relish.
YIELD: 3 half-pints.
NOTE: Wear disposable gloves when working with jalapeño peppers.

Freezing and Canning

Kosher Dill Pickles

4 lb. (4") pickling cucumbers
14 cloves garlic, peeled
    & cut in half
1/4 c. pickling salt
3 c. water

2 3/4 c. vinegar (5%
    acidity)
14 sprigs fresh dill weed
28 peppercorns

WASH cucumbers, and cut in half lengthwise.
COMBINE garlic, salt, water and vinegar; bring to a boil.
REMOVE garlic and place 4 halves into each hot, sterilized jar.
PACK cucumbers into jars, adding 2 sprigs dill weed and 4 peppercorns to each jar.
POUR boiling vinegar mixture over cucumbers, leaving 1/2-inch headspace.
REMOVE air bubbles; wipe jar rims.
COVER jars at once with metal lids, and screw on metal bands.
PROCESS jars in boiling-water bath 10 minutes.
YIELD: 6 to 7 pints.

Lime Pickles

8 lb. cucumbers, sliced
    (1/4" slices)

2 c. white lime
2 gal. water

COVER cucumbers with liquid, let stand for 24 hours.
POUR off and rinse well.
COVER with fresh cold water. Let soak 3 hours; drain.
MIX together with the following:

2 qt. vinegar
8 c. white vinegar
1 T. salt

1 tsp. celery seed
1 tsp. whole cloves
1 tsp. mixed pickling spices

WITH above, add enough water to cover pickles; let stand overnight.
BOIL gently 30 to 40 minutes.
PACK in jars and seal.
YOU may add green food coloring, if desired.
YIELD: 5 to 6 pints.

Freezing and Canning

Mixed Citrus Marmalade

4 1/2 qt. water, divided
1 1/2 c. thinly-sliced grape-
    fruit rind
1/2 c. thinly-sliced orange
    rind

1 1/2 c. chopped grape-
    fruit sections
3/4 c. chopped orange
    sections
1/2 c. thinly-sliced lemon
About 2 1/2 c. sugar

COMBINE 1 1/2 quarts water, grapefruit rind and orange rind in a large Dutch oven; bring to a boil. Boil, uncovered, 5 minutes; drain. Repeat procedure.

COMBINE remaining 1 1/2 quarts water, boiled rind, chopped fruit and lemon slices; bring mixture to a boil, and boil 5 minutes. Cover and let stand 12 to 18 hours in a cool place.

UNCOVER, bring mixture to a boil, and boil 35 to 40 minutes, or until rind is tender. Measure amount of fruit and liquid; add 1 cup sugar per 1 cup fruit and liquid. Stir well. Bring mixture to a boil, and boil until mixture registers 221° on a candy thermometer, stirring frequently.

POUR boiling marmalade into hot, sterilized jars, leaving 1/4-inch headspace; wipe jar rims. Cover at once with metal lids, and screw on bands.

PROCESS in boiling-water bath for 10 minutes.

YIELD: 3 half-pints.

Freezing and Canning

Mom's Two-Week Sweet Pickles

3 1/2 qt. (2") pickling
    cucumbers (4 lb.)
1 c. coarse pickling salt
2 qt. boiling water
1/2 tsp. powdered alum
5 c. vinegar

3 c. sugar
1 1/2 tsp. celery seeds
4 (2") sticks cinnamon
1 tsp. whole cloves
1 1/2 c. sugar

WASH cucumbers carefully; cut in lengthwise halves, or leave whole, prick with fork and place in stone crock, glass, pottery or enamel-lined (unchipped) pan.

PREPARE brine by dissolving salt in boiling water; pour over cucumbers. Weight cucumbers down with a plate almost as large as the crock, and lay a stone or paraffin brick (not marble or limestone) on plate to keep cucumbers under brine. Let stand 1 week.

ON the eighth day, drain; pour 2 quarts fresh boiling water over the cucumbers. Let stand 24 hours.

ON the ninth day, drain; pour 2 quarts fresh boiling water, mixed with alum, over cucumbers. Let stand 24 hours.

ON the tenth day, drain; pour 2 quarts fresh boiling water over cucumbers. Let stand 24 hours.

THE next day, drain. Combine vinegar, 3 cups sugar, celery seeds and cinnamon; heat to boiling point and pour over cucumbers.

FOR the next 3 days, drain, retaining liquid. Reheat this liquid each morning, adding 1/2 cup sugar each time. After the last heating, on the 14th day, pack pickles into hot jars. Remove cinnamon sticks and cloves; pour boiling hot liquid over pickles; adjust lids.

PROCESS in boiling water bath 5 minutes. Remove jars and retighten lids, leave to seal.

YIELD: 5 to 6 pints.

YOU may make these pickles in larger amounts by adjusting amounts, and following the same directions.

Freezing and Canning

Okra Pickles

3 1/2 lb. sm. okra pods
7 cloves garlic
7 sm. fresh hot peppers

2 c. vinegar (5% acidity)
1/3 c. pickling salt
2 tsp. dill seeds

PACK okra tightly into hot sterilized jars, leaving 1/2-inch headspace; place a large clove and a hot pepper in each.
COMBINE water, vinegar, pickling salt and dill seeds in a saucepan; bring to a boil.
POUR boiling vinegar mixture over okra, leaving 1/2-inch headspace.
REMOVE air bubbles; wipe jar rims.
COVER at once with metal lids, and screw on bands.
PROCESS in boiling water bath 10 minutes.
YIELD: 7 pints.

Peach Pickles

3 qt. cold water
3/4 tsp. ascorbic-citric
    powder
8 lb. sm. to med.-size firm,
    ripe peaches, peeled

6 3/4 c. sugar
1 qt. vinegar (5% acidity)
4 (3") sticks cinnamon
2 T. whole cloves
1 (1") piece ginger root

COMBINE water and ascorbic-citric powder in a large container. Drop peaches in water mixture; set aside.
COMBINE sugar and vinegar in a large Dutch oven; bring to a boil, and cook 5 minutes. Tie remaining ingredients in a cheesecloth bag, and add to syrup.
DRAIN peaches and add to syrup mixture. Cook, uncovered, about 3 minutes or just until peaches can be pierced with a fork. Remove from heat. Cover and let stand at room temperature for 24 hours.
BRING peaches to a boil; pack hot peaches into hot sterilized jars, leaving 1/2-inch headspace. Pour boiling syrup over peaches, leaving 1/2-inch headspace. Remove air bubbles; wipe jar rims. Cover at once with metal lids, and screw on bands. Process in boiling water bath 15 minutes.
YIELD: 6 pints.

Freezing and Canning

Peach Preserves

3 lb. peaches, peeled &
   quartered
4 c. sugar
1 c. honey

1/2 med.-size orange,
   quartered & seeded
1/2 tsp. salt (opt.)
1/4 tsp. almond extract

COMBINE peaches, sugar and honey in a large Dutch oven. Cover and let stand about 45 minutes.

POSITION knife blade in food processor bowl. Add orange and top with cover. Process until finely chopped. Measure orange, and add an equal amount of water. Cover and cook over medium heat, about 10 minutes, or until orange peel is soft.

BRING peaches slowly to a boil, stirring frequently, until sugar dissolves. Bring to a rapid boil, and cook 15 minutes, stirring constantly. Add orange mixture, return to a boil, and cook about 25 minutes, or until mixture registers 221° on a candy thermometer; stir mixture frequently. Remove from heat; stir in salt, if desired, and almond extract.

SKIM off foam with a metal spoon.

SPOON hot preserves into hot jars, leaving 1/4-inch headspace; wipe jar rims. Cover with metal lids, screw on bands.

PROCESS in boiling water bath 15 minutes.

YIELD: 5 half-pints.

Pepper Jelly

1 1/2 c. minced green pepper
1/2 c. minced hot green
   pepper

7 1/2 c. sugar
1 1/2 c. vinegar (5% acidity)
2 (3 oz.) pkg. liquid pectin

COMBINE first 4 ingredients in a Dutch oven; bring to a boil. Boil 6 minutes, stirring frequently. Stir in pectin; boil 3 minutes, stirring frequently. Remove from heat and skim off foam with a metal spoon.

QUICKLY pour hot jelly into hot, sterilized jars, leaving 1/4-inch headspace; wipe jar rims. Cover at once with metal lids, and screw on bands.

PROCESS in boiling-water bath 5 minutes.

YIELD: 7 half-pints.

Freezing and Canning

Pepper Relish

6 green peppers, minced	2 c. vinegar (5% acidity)
6 sweet red peppers, minced	1 1/2 c. sugar
6 med. onions, minced	2 T. + 1 tsp. mustard seeds
1 hot pepper	

COMBINE all ingredients in a large Dutch oven, and bring to a boil. Reduce heat to medium; cook, uncovered, 30 minutes, stirring occasionally. Discard hot pepper.

QUICKLY spoon hot relish into hot, sterilized jars, leaving 1/4-inch headspace. Remove air bubbles; wipe jar rims. Cover at once with metal lids, and screw on bands. Process in boiling-water bath 10 minutes.

YIELD: 10 half-pints.

Perfect Mincemeat

THIS recipe may be reduced to suit your needs.

12 lb. apples	1/2 c. lemon juice
3 lb. lean beef, cooked	1 c. orange juice
1 lb. suet	3 c. water
3 lb. seedless raisins	1 c. sliced citron peel
4 c. sugar	1 T. ground cloves
2 c. brown sugar	1 T. salt
2 T. cinnamon	1/2 c. cider vinegar
2 c. white corn syrup	

PEEL apples and grind with beef and suet; add the remaining ingredients and cook, covered, in a large kettle over medium-low heat for 30 minutes.

UNCOVER, and continue cooking until desired consistency, about 1 hour.

PROCESS 1 hour and 30 minutes in hot water bath.

YIELD: According to how large a batch you make.

Freezing and Canning

Pickled Beets

8 to 9 lb. sm. fresh beets
1 T. mustard seeds
1 tsp. celery seeds

3 1/2 c. vinegar (5% acidity)
3 c. sugar
1 1/2 tsp. pickling salt

LEAVE root and 1-inch of stem on beets; scrub with a brush. Place beets in a saucepan; add water to cover. Bring to a boil; cover, reduce heat and simmer 35 to 40 minutes, or until tender. Drain, reserving 2 1/2 cups liquid; pour cold water over beets and drain. Trim off beet root and stems; then rub off skins. Set beets aside.
COMBINE mustard seeds and celery seeds in a cheesecloth bag. Combine vinegar, reserved beet liquid, sugar, pickling salt and spice bag in a Dutch oven. Bring mixture to a boil; reduce heat and simmer 15 minutes.
PACK beets into hot jars, leaving 1/2-inch headspace. Pour boiling syrup over beets, leaving 1/2-inch headspace. Remove air bubbles; wipe jar rims. Cover at once with metal lids, and screw on bands. Process in boiling-water bath 30 minutes.
YIELD: 7 pints.

Quick Grape Jelly

2 c. bottled unsweetened
   grape juice

3 1/2 c. sugar
1 (3 oz.) pkg. liquid pectin

COMBINE grape juice and sugar in a large Dutch oven; bring to a boil, stirring constantly. Remove from heat, and skim off foam with a metal spoon.
QUICKLY pour hot jelly into hot, sterilized jars, leaving 1/2-inch headspace; wipe jar rims. Cover at once with metal lids, and screw on bands.
PROCESS in boiling-water bath 5 minutes.
YIELD: 4 half-pints.

Freezing and Canning

Raspberry-Plum Jam

4 1/2 c. chopped or coarsely-
  ground pitted plums
  (about 2 1/2 lb.)
2 (10 oz. each) pkg. frozen
  raspberries in syrup,
  thawed

10 c. sugar
1/2 c. lemon juice
2 pouches (3 oz. each) liquid
  fruit pectin

IN a large kettle, combine plums, raspberries, sugar and lemon juice. Bring to a full rolling boil over high heat, stirring constantly. Quickly stir in pectin; return to a full rolling boil. Boil for 1 minute, stirring constantly.
REMOVE from the heat; skim off any foam.
POUR hot into hot jars, leaving 1/4-inch headspace.
ADJUST caps.
PROCESS in a boiling-water bath for 15 minutes.

Rhubarb Jam

5 c. diced rhubarb

5 c. sugar

DISSOLVE sugar with rhubarb, one cup at a time, and bring to boil; boil 10 minutes.
REMOVE from heat and add 1 package cherry or strawberry Jello.
POUR into sterilized jars and seal.

Freezing and Canning

Shortcut Chili Sauce

3 qt. peeled tomatoes	2 c. sugar
3 c. chopped celery	1/4 c. brown sugar
2 c. chopped onions	1 1/2 tsp. pepper
1 c. chopped green pepper	1 1/2 tsp. mixed pickling spices
1/4 c. salt	1 c. white vinegar

COMBINE tomatoes, celery, onion, green pepper and salt. Let stand overnight. Drain in colander, but do not press vegetables.
PLACE vegetable mixture in large kettle and add sugars, pepper, pickling spices tied in a cheesecloth bag, and vinegar. Bring to a boil; reduce heat and simmer, uncovered, 15 minutes. Remove spices.
LADLE into hot jars; adjust lids.
PROCESS in a boiling-water bath 10 minutes.
REMOVE jars and retighten lids.
YIELD: 5 1/2 pints.

Spiced Apple Sticks

12 med. apples, peeled & cored	1/2 c. light corn syrup
3 qt. water	1 c. vinegar
3 T. vinegar	2 tsp. whole cloves
1 c. sugar	1 1/2 sticks cinnamon

CUT apples into eighths and cover with water and vinegar.
COMBINE all other ingredients in a kettle. Bring slowly to a boil.
ADD well-drained apples; cover and boil 3 minutes, stirring constantly.
PACK apple sticks in hot jars and cover with liquid; adjust lids.
Process in boiling-water bath 15 minutes.
REMOVE jars from canner and complete seals.
YIELD: 4 pints.

Freezing and Canning

Strawberry Marmalade

2 med. oranges	1 qt. ripe strawberries,
2 med. lemons	crushed
1/2 c. water	7 c. sugar
1/8 tsp. baking soda	1 pouch liquid fruit pectin,
	(half of a 6 oz. pkg.)

PEEL outer layer of oranges and lemons; set aside.

REMOVE the white membrane from fruit and discard. Set the fruit aside.

CHOP peels; place in a large saucepan. Add water and baking soda; cover and bring to a boil. Simmer for 10 minutes.

MEANWHILE, section oranges and lemons, reserving juice. Add fruit and juice to saucepan; cover and simmer 20 minutes. Add strawberries.

MEASURE fruit; return 4 cups to the saucepan. (If you have more than 4 cups, discard any extra; if less, add water to equal 4 cups.)

ADD the sugar and mix well. Boil, uncovered, for 5 minutes.

REMOVE from the heat; stir in pectin. Stir for 5 minutes to cool; skim off foam.

POUR into half-pint jars or freezer containers, leaving 1/4-inch headspace.

ADJUST caps.

PROCESS for 10 minutes in boiling-water bath or store in the freezer.

YIELD: 10 half-pints.

Freezing and Canning

Strawberry Preserves

1 1/2 pt. sm. strawberries
5 c. sugar
1/3 c. lemon juice

WASH and hull strawberries. Combine strawberries and sugar in a large Dutch oven; stir well and let mixture stand 3 to 4 hours.

SLOWLY bring strawberry mixture to a boil, stirring occasionally, until sugar dissolves. Stir in lemon juice. Boil about 12 minutes, or until berries are clear, stirring occasionally. Remove from heat, and skim off foam with a metal spoon.

CAREFULLY remove fruit from the syrup with a slotted spoon, and place in a shallow pan. Bring syrup to a boil; cook about 10 minutes, or until syrup has thickened to desired consistency. Pour syrup over fruit. Cover loosely with paper towels, and let stand 12 to 24 hours in a cool place. Shake pan occasionally (do not stir) so berries will absorb syrup and remain plump. Skim off foam with a metal spoon.

HEAT mixture in Dutch oven, and ladle hot preserves into hot jars, leaving 1/4-inch headspace; wipe jar rims. Cover at once with metal lids, and screw on bands.

PROCESS in boiling water bath 20 minutes.

YIELD: 4 half-pints.

Strawberry-Rhubarb Jam

2 1/2 c. fresh strawberries
(may use frozen)
1 1/2 c. finely-diced fresh
rhubarb (may use frozen)
2 1/2 c. sugar
1 (8 oz.) can crushed
pineapple, undrained
1 (3 oz.) pkg. strawberry-
flavored gelatin

IN a large kettle, combine strawberries, rhubarb, sugar and pineapple. Bring to a boil; reduce heat and simmer for 20 minutes. Remove from heat; stir in gelatin until dissolved.

POUR into jars or freezer containers, leaving 1/2-inch headspace. COOL.

TOP with lids; refrigerate or freeze.

YIELD: 5 1/2 cups.

Freezing and Canning

Sweet Dill Pickles

6 cucumbers
Ice water
Onion slices or clove of
    garlic
Dill, fresh or dried

1 c. sugar
1 c. water
1 pt. vinegar
1/3 c. salt

SOAK whole cucumbers in ice water 3 to 4 hours. Drain. Slice or cut into strips. Place in hot jars along with onions and a generous amount of dill.

COMBINE sugar, water, vinegar and salt; bring to a boil. Pour over pickles to within 1/2-inch from jar top. Adjust lids. Process in boiling water bath 20 minutes (start to count the processing time as soon as hot jars are placed into the actively boiling water). Remove jars from canner and complete seals.

YIELD: 3 pints.

Sweet Pickle Relish

4 c. chopped cucumbers
2 c. chopped onion
1 green pepper, chopped
1 sweet red pepper, chopped
1/4 c. pickling salt

1 3/4 c. sugar
1 c. cider vinegar (5%
    acidity)
1 1/2 tsp. celery seed
1 1/2 tsp. mustard seeds

COMBINE first 4 ingredients; sprinkle with salt, and cover with cold water. Let stand 2 hours; drain.

COMBINE sugar, vinegar and spices in a large Dutch oven; bring to a boil, and add vegetables. Return to a boil; reduce heat, and simmer 10 minutes.

PACK hot mixture into sterilized jars, leaving 1/4-inch headspace. Remove air bubbles; wipe jar rims. Cover at once with metal lids, and screw on bands.

PROCESS in boiling-water bath 10 minutes.

YIELD: 4 half-pints.

Freezing and Canning

Tomato Relish

32 med. tomatoes, about 16 lb.	3 T. salt
12 med. onions, finely chopped	2 c. firmly-packed brown sugar
3 red peppers, finely chopped	2 c. vinegar (5% acidity)
3 green peppers, finely chopped	1 T. ground cinnamon
	1 1/2 tsp. ground allspice
	1 1/2 tsp. ground cloves

PEEL, core and chop tomatoes.

COMBINE tomatoes and next 4 ingredients in a large kettle. Bring to a boil; reduce heat to medium and cook, uncovered, 25 minutes. Add remaining ingredients; reduce heat and simmer, uncovered, 1 1/2 to 2 hours, or until thickened.

QUICKLY pack hot mixture into hot, sterilized jars, leaving 1/2-inch headspace. Remove air bubbles; wipe jar rims. Cover at once with metal lids, and screw on bands. Process in boiling water bath 10 minutes. YIELD: 12 pints.

Uncooked Tomato Relish

18 med. tomatoes	1/3 c. salt
2 branches celery	2 1/2 c. sugar
2 green peppers	1/2 tsp. pepper
2 sweet red peppers	1/2 tsp. ground cinnamon
4 med. onions	3 T. whole mustard seeds
1/2 c. finely-ground horseradish	3 c. cider vinegar

SCALD tomatoes; remove skins and as many seeds as possible. Chop into small pieces; should make about 3 quarts chopped tomatoes.

PUT celery, peppers and onions through food chopper, using coarse grind. Use the finest grind for horseradish.

COMBINE vegetables and salt; let stand overnight in refrigerator. Drain thoroughly in a strainer. Add sugar, spices, mustard seeds and vinegar; mix well.

PACK in hot jars; seal and store in refrigerator. Should keep for several months. (Do not store at room temperature.) YIELD: 4 quarts.

THIS makes a great topping for meat loaf, or may be served with any meat.

Freezing and Canning

Watermelon Rind Pickles

1 lg. watermelon, quartered
Pickling salt
2 T. + 2 tsp. whole cloves
16 (1 1/2") sticks cinnamon

1/2 tsp. mustard seeds
8 c. sugar
1 qt. vinegar (5% acidity)

REMOVE flesh from melon (reserve for other uses); peel watermelon. Cut rind into 1-inch cubes.
PLACE rind in a large crock or plastic container. Add water by the quart until it covers the rind; add 1/4 cup pickling salt for each quart, stirring until salt dissolves. Cover and let stand in a cool place 8 hours; drain well.
PLACE rind in a 10-quart Dutch oven; cover with cold water. Bring to a boil, and boil until rind is almost tender. Drain and set aside.
TIE cloves, cinnamon and mustard seeds in a cheesecloth bag. Combine spice bag, sugar and vinegar in a Dutch oven. Bring to a boil, remove from heat, and let stand 15 minutes. Add rind to syrup. Bring to a boil; reduce heat to low and cook until rind is transparent. Remove spice bag.
PACK hot rind into hot sterilized jars; fill with hot liquid, leaving 1/2-inch headspace. Remove air bubbles; wipe jar rims. Cover jars at once with metal lids and screw on metal bands. Process jars in boiling water bath 10 minutes. Yield: 5 pints.

Zucchini-Pineapple Jam

6 c. seeded, shredded,
    zucchini
6 c. sugar
1/2 c. lemon juice

1 (20 oz.) can crushed
    pineapple, undrained
1 (6 oz.) pkg. strawberry-
    flavored gelatin

IN a large kettle, bring the zucchini and sugar to a boil. Boil and stir constantly for 6 minutes. Add the lemon juice and pineapple; cook and stir for 8 minutes. Add gelatin; stir for 1 minute.
REMOVE from heat.
SKIM off any foam; fill jars or plastic containers.
COOL before covering with lids.
REFRIGERATE up to 3 weeks.
YIELD: 8 1/2 cups.

Freezing and Canning

Zucchini Relish

10 c. ground zucchini,
(peeling but not seeding)
4 lg. onions, ground

4 red peppers, ground
4 green peppers, ground

PUT a handful of salt over and let stand overnight. It will get very juicy; drain.
COMBINE:

2 1/2 c. vinegar
4 c. sugar
1 tsp. turmeric

1 tsp. nutmeg
2 tsp. celery seed
2 T. cornstarch

BOIL together; then add zucchini and simmer about 20 minutes.
PUT into jars and seal.
YIELD: about 6 to 8 pints.

Freezing and Canning

Information About Chili Peppers

STORAGE: Store fresh chilies in the refrigerator in a plastic bag left slightly open (allowing air for the peppers to "breathe"). Peppers need to be kept free of moisture. If you wash the peppers ahead of time, remember to pat dry, using a paper towel. Peppers should be used within 5 to 7 days.

FREEZING: Whole or chopped, chili peppers can also be frozen in airtight bags. Frozen peppers will last in the refrigerator up to 6 months in the freezer.

PREPARATION: Remove the stem and slit the pod in half lengthwise. Slide a butter knife along the inside of the pepper and remove the seeds (removing the seeds evens the heat and allows a smoother heat distribution).

ROASTING a fresh chili pepper: Some peppers, such as poblano and New Mexico, are often roasted or grilled prior to using in a recipe. Place the pods over an open flame or grill, or beneath a broiler, for 4 to 6 minutes on each side until the skin is charred and puffy. (Pulling out the chilies' core and seeds before roasting is optional.) Remove the chilies from the heat and let cool for a few minutes. Scrape the thin layer of charred skin and discard. Remove the remaining seeds and chop or slice the pepper as you desire.

IF you have sensitive skin, it is best to wear rubber gloves when handling peppers. Avoid touching any part of your face. You will notice a very unpleasant burning sensation.

TO relieve too hot food for your taste, dairy products work best. Water or cola seem to cause the heat to increase.

Freezing and Canning

Fresh Chili Peppers

CAYENNE CHILI PEPPERS are long, narrow chilies with a peppery heat. Cayennes are often dried and ground into powders and processed into bottled hot sauces, the fresh pods are favorites in soups and chili. They are used as a flavor in Creole, African and Indian cuisines.

CHERRY PEPPERS are a small bulbous pepper with a mild to tingly heat.

CONGO PEPPERS are used in curry dishes, stews, marinades and many tropical hot sauces.

HABANEROS are lantern-shaped, colorful pods with <u>ferocious</u> heat and an apricot aroma. They are regarded as one of the world's hottest peppers. Habaneros are used in salsas, soups, chilies and bisques, and are used in many bottled hot sauces.

HUNGARIAN WAX PEPPERS are often called yellow wax hots. They are yellow to pale-green peppers with the shape of a small contorted banana. They are medium-to-hot in the heat range. They have a slight citrus flavor. They are used in salsas, soups and gazpacho. Mild wax peppers are called banana peppers.

JALAPEÑOS are thick-fleshed chilies shaped like bullets. They range from mild to hot, and dark green to deep red. They are perhaps the most versatile pepper, and are used in salsas, chilies, soups, stews, bean and rice dishes, marinades, and breads.
Jalapeños are also available canned, pickled, and smoked and dried (under the name of chipotle).

NEW MEXICO PEPPERS are long, tapered chilies, green and red with a fruity heat, and aromatic flavor. They are always roasted before use, to soften the flesh and remove the outer skin. They may be dried, and are ground into sauces and powders.

Freezing and Canning

PEPPERONCINIS are pickled, yellowish-green Italian peppers with a mild heat. These peppers are also found on salad bars. They are used in dressings, salads, bean dishes, grain salads, red sauces and antipasto.

POBLANOS are large, greenish-purple pods with an anvil shape, sturdy skin, raisiny flavor and medium-to-hot heat. They are often roasted before using. They are one of the most popular chilies in Mexico and the Southwest.
Dried poblanos are marketed as ancho chilies.

RED FRESNOS are similar to red jalapeños, but display slightly more heat. They are interchangeable with the jalapeños.

ROCATILLOS (aji dulce) are tiny, multicolored chilies with a squash shape. They have a sweet, citrusy flavor and mild heat.

SCOTCH BONNET PEPPERS have very, very hot heat. They originate in Jamaica, and have a rainbow of colors. They are used in jerk sauce, soups, stews, rice-and-bean dishes, and many bottled hot sauces. They are also known as country peppers, bonneys, and Bahama mamas. Scotch bonnets are interchangeable with habaneros.

SEASONING PEPPERS are neon-colored, curry pods with a citrusy, sweet flavor and tingly heat.
They are not available in the United States.

SERRANOS are narrow, pointy peppers with a sharp, prickly heat. The pod is dense with seeds, with contribute to its concentrated degree of heat. Serranos come in green, red and reddish-orange colors. They are used in soups, stews, chilies, curries, salsas and stir-fries.
Serranos are interchangeable with hot jalapeños, cayenne chili peppers and red Fresnos.

TABASCO PEPPERS are small, cone-shaped chilies with a rather forceful heat. It is best known for its use in Louisiana hot sauce, in which the peppers are mashed, fermented and aged.
Tabasco hot sauce is considered to be the world's most popular hot sauce.

Freezing and Canning

Information on Dried Chilies

UNLIKE fresh chilies, dried chilies have a long shelf life (if properly stored). Dried chilies require different preparation than fresh chilies. They may be toasted in an ungreased skillet for a few minutes before adding to a recipe. The dried pods are seared and turned for about 2 minutes, and then covered with simmering hot water and soaked until they are soft, about 15 to 20 minutes. The chilies can then be added to a soup or stew, or puréed with a little soaking liquid and transformed into a thick paste. Another popular method calls for toasting the chilies and grinding them into a spice powder.

ANCHOS are dried green poblano peppers with wide shoulders and a burnt-red, brownish hue. It has a musky, raisiny flavor and is used in sauces (mole), salsas, and chili-stews. ("Ancho" means "broad" or "wide" in Spanish.)

BIRD PEPPERS, also known as pequin and chiltepin, are tiny, ovoid peppers with a firecracker (but fleeting) heat. The reddish-orange, berry-like pods have grown wild in the Caribbean for centuries.

CASCABELS are cherry mahogany-colored chilies with a smoky flavor and a small, bulbous shape. "Casabel" meals "rattle" or "jingle" in Spanish (the dried pods make a rattling sound when shaken).

CAYENNE CHILI PEPPERS are long, thin peppers with a "bite". They are often ground and sold as a powder or processed into bottled hot sauces. Typically, the generic ground red pepper found in stores is made with cayennes.

CHILI DE ARBOLS are long, narrow pods with a reddish-orange hue, thin skin, and intense heat. They are similar to cayenne peppers.

CHIPOTLES are large jalapeño peppers that have been dried and smoked. They are available canned in a spicy adobo sauce or air-packed in bags. Soak the air-packed chilies for 20 minutes in warm water before using. Chipotles have a dark brownish-red color, smoky flavor, and piercing heat.

Freezing and Canning

GUAJILLOS are long, slender pods with a shiny, reddish-mahogany tint and fruity, almost tart flavor. They are one of the most popular chilies used in Mexican cooking.

NEW MEXICOS, when dried, turn brick-red and develop a tangy, zesty flavor. They are used in red chili sauces, chili-stews, posoles, and spicy soups. Dried they are ground into sauces or powders and are also tied into holiday wreaths (called ristras) and displayed as ornaments.

Information on Hot Sauces

THERE is a vast array of hot sauces and chili pastes. They are available, including jalapeño sauces, sweet sambals, potent Thai curry pastes, and fiery Scotch Bonnet pepper sauces. More and more cooks are using hot sauce or spice paste.

CHILI-GARLIC PASTE is a thick, brick-red sauce of red chilies, vinegar, garlic and Asian spices.

HABANERO AND SCOTCH BONNET PEPPER SAUCES contain puréed chilies, vinegar, and/or citrus juice, tropical fruits and occasionally sugar or mustard. These sauces can be red, green or yellow, they should have a fruity flavor, blistering heat, and thick (not runny) consistency.

HARISSA is a brick-red spice paste called for in Moroccan recipes. Cumin, coriander, red chili peppers and paprika are the core ingredients. Harissa is similar to a liquid chili powder.

SAMBAL is an Indonesian chili paste with a flavorful "sweet heat" sensation. Serve with rice dishes or as a flavoring paste for soups and stews.

TABASCO and other LOUISIANA HOT SAUCES are piquant, vinegary liquids made from the fermented mash of Tabasco peppers or cayenne chili peppers, depending on the brand.

THAI CURRY PASTE is a wet paste of chilies, herbs and Asian spices typically sold in small cans or plastic pouches. Curry paste, when combined with coconut milk, forms the basis of most Thai curry dishes.

Freezing and Canning

Hot Salsa

10 c. chopped cherry tomatoes
3 c. chopped onion
1 to 2 c. chopped garlic
1/2 to 1 bunch fresh
    cilantro, chopped
16 sm. jalapeño peppers,
    chopped
1 c. cider vinegar
3 1/2 tsp. salt

CHOP cherry tomatoes in food processor. Add onions, garlic, cilantro and jalapeño peppers and pulse to mix well.
PUT processed vegetables in a large kettle and add cider vinegar and salt. Bring ingredients to a full boil. Simmer for additional 15 minutes.
POUR cooked ingredients into hot, sterilized jars. Fill to within 1/4-inch of top. Place in boiling water bath for 15 minutes.
YIELD: 7 or 8 pints.
YOU may change the intensity of the heat in this sauce, for a milder sauce, remove all the seeds from the jalapeño peppers. For a medium-hot sauce, remove half the seeds.
CHERRY tomatoes give a sweet flavor, but you may use regular tomatoes.

Salsa

4 c. coarsely-chopped,
    peeled tomatoes
1 c. chopped onion
1 c. chopped jalapeño
    peppers
1 c. chopped sweet cherry
    peppers
1 (15 oz.) can tomato sauce
1 (16 oz.) jar mild picante sauce
1 c. cider vinegar

BRING all ingredients to a boil in a glass nonaluminum pan. Stir with a wooden spoon.
SIMMER for about 1 1/2 hours.
POUR hot vegetable mixture into hot, sterilized jars. Process and seal according to jar manufacturer's directions.
THIS sauce has a really great flavor when prepared with homegrown tomatoes and jalapeños.
FOR a milder sauce, remove seeds from half the peppers.
TO peel tomatoes easily, blanch in boiling water for 10 to 15 seconds, or until skin pops, then plunge into chilled water.

Freezing and Canning

Salsa Dressing

2 ripe tomatoes, peeled
1/2 sm. onion, minced
1/2 to 1 fresh jalapeño
   pepper, seeds removed
   & minced

1/2 to 1 tsp. salt
1 tsp. fresh lime juice
1/2 tsp. vegetable oil
1/2 tsp. vinegar

COMBINE all ingredients in a food processor.
PULSE to salsa consistency; do not purée.

Hawaiian Salsa

1 c. chopped pineapple
1 mango, peeled & chopped
1 papaya, peeled & chopped
1 med.-sized green bell
   pepper, chopped
2 kiwi, peeled & chopped

1/2 c. chopped purple onion
1/4 c. chopped cilantro
2 mild jalapeño peppers,
   seeds removed & chopped
Juice of 1 lime
Ground white pepper, to taste

MIX all ingredients well; chill before use.
THIS salsa is great served with pork chops or fish fillets.

PORK TENDERLOINS:
   4 oz. pork tenderloins

GRILL pork tenderloins over medium-hot coals 6 to 8 minutes on
each side, or until juice runs clear, or desired doneness.
REMOVE from grill and serve with salsa.

Freezing and Canning

Papaya Corn Salsa

1/2 fresh papaya, peeled,
   & diced
1/4 c. minced red bell
   pepper
1/4 c. minced purple onion

1/2 c. cooked, fresh,
   frozen or canned corn
1 sm. avocado, chopped
3 T. lime juice
1 T. olive oil
1/4 tsp. salt

COMBINE all ingredients; mix and chill.
THIS salsa is delicious served with fish.
SUGGESTED fish: Halibut steaks.
MIX:

1/2 tsp. salt
1/4 tsp. ground white pepper

1/2 tsp. crumbled or
   ground thyme

BRUSH fish with olive oil on both sides.
SEASON with spice mix of salt, pepper and thyme.
GRILL over medium-hot coals for 10 to 12 minutes, turning several times.
REMOVE from grill and serve with salsa.

Freezing and Canning

ORDER BLANK

NAME _____

ADDRESS _____

CITY & STATE _____ ZIP _____

How many copies? _____ Amount enclosed _____
    Price per book $12.00
    Postage & handling 2.50
    Total $14.50
Please make checks payable to:
                  The Machine Shed
Mail orders to: From Planting to Pickling
                  111 W. 76th Street
                  Davenport, IA 52806

ORDER BLANK

NAME _____

ADDRESS _____

CITY & STATE _____ ZIP _____

How many copies? _____ Amount enclosed _____
    Price per book $12.00
    Postage & handling 2.50
    Total $14.50
Please make checks payable to:
                  The Machine Shed
Mail orders to: From Planting to Pickling
                  111 W. 76th Street
                  Davenport, IA 52806

ORDER BLANK

NAME _____

ADDRESS _____

CITY & STATE _____ ZIP _____

How many copies? _____ Amount enclosed _____
    Price per book $12.00
    Postage & handling 2.50
    Total $14.50
Please make checks payable to:
                  The Machine Shed
Mail orders to: From Planting to Pickling
                  111 W. 76th Street
                  Davenport, IA 52806